Praise for *A Path to Belonging*

"*A Path to Belonging* is an important co
of clergy and congregational well-bei
final two chapters are a reminder to thos   ...s in congregational and denominational leadership of our role in helping
our pastors get the support they need, which in turn benefits
the whole congregational system."

—Susan Nienaber, district superintendent, Minnesota
Annual Conference of the United Methodist Church

"*A Path to Belonging* conveys a profound understanding of
the extent to which clergy express loneliness, a crisis revealed
in their feeling isolated and alone even while ministering in
community. DuChene and Sundby offer exceptional insight
into how hard it is to care for others when we can't give our
best in the midst of our own loneliness. Our synod highly
recommends this must-have resource for clergy and those
who equip and support them as they exercise their spiritual
abilities and effective leadership during extraordinary times."

—Elona Street-Stewart, ruling elder, synod executive of the
Synod of Lakes and Prairies and co-moderator of the 224th
General Assembly of the Presbyterian Church (U.S.A.)

"This book speaks to the hearts of clergy! Even in the best of times, clergy leaders inherently feel isolated and lonely. DuChene and Sunbdy share stories, studies, and reflections to help us better understand these feelings and then suggest ways to work through them toward a greater awareness of well-being. I will be recommending this book to our clergy."

—Karen Olson, canon for ministry in the Episcopal Church in Minnesota

"In *A Path to Belonging: Overcoming Clergy Loneliness*, DuChene and Sundby provide rich, detailed, and deeply valuable guidance for the journey from depleting, soul- and body-destroying clergy loneliness to balanced care for one's congregation and oneself. Through multiple case examples and self-care methods, they offer readers hope of a satisfying life—caring for others' religious and spiritual needs while experiencing joy, health, and connection to others."

—Thomas Skovholt, University of Minnesota, and co-author of The Resilient Practitioner, third edition a path to belonging

a
path
to
belonging

overcoming
clergy loneliness

Mary Kay DuChene
Mark Sundby

Fortress Press
Minneapolis

A PATH TO BELONGING
Overcoming Clergy Loneliness

Cover design: Laurie Ingram Art + Design.com
Cover image: Photography/Horstgerlach/iStock

Print ISBN: 978-1-5064-7381-9
eBook ISBN: 978-1-5064-7382-6

To all LeaderWise clergy clients,
We see you: brave, holy, and human

Contents

Preface   ix

Acknowledgments   xi

Introduction   1

PART I. THE EPIDEMIC OF LONELINESS   11

1. What Is Loneliness?   13

2. The Impact of Loneliness   25

3. The Clergy Life   37

PART II. PATHS TO BELONGING   61

4. Learning to Think Differently   65

5. The Essentials of Belonging   83

6. The Spirituality Connection   109

7. Being Wise about Loneliness   129

8. Resilience Matters   141

Contents

PART III. FOR CONGREGATIONS,
DENOMINATIONS, AND JUDICATORIES   153

9. What Congregations Can Do   155

10. A Word to Denominations and Judicatories   165

Appendix: LeaderWise Clergy Loneliness Survey   173

Notes   177

Recommended Resources   185

Preface

We, Mark and Mary Kay, are colleagues at LeaderWise, which is a 501c3 nonprofit organization that serves people in lives of service, primarily ministers and their congregations. We provide counseling, coaching, spiritual direction, consulting, pastoral supervision, and leadership development experiences.

In our work, we have seen the effects loneliness has had on clergy, especially in the last few years, and it is for that reason that we have felt compelled to write this book. The genesis of the idea came before the pandemic, and the pandemic only increased the urgency of the work, even as our day-to-day work also intensified as we accompanied people through the turbulent times we are experiencing.

In this book, we use the terms *clergy* or *minister* to describe our audience. There are many names for those we are including in these terms: pastors, priests, rabbis, imams, deacons, deaconesses, chaplains, commissioned lay ministers, and ministers of all other kinds. Many of the stories in this book lift up people we think of as "pastors," simply because they are the people with whom we work the most. But ministers of all types experience loneliness in ministry, and this book is for and about all of you and them.

At LeaderWise, we strive to base our consulting and counseling practice on empirical science, and the same holds true for this book. As part of our research, we conducted a national survey of clergy loneliness using the UCLA Loneliness Scale (Version 3), which is the most widely used survey in contemporary loneliness research. We also held three ninety-minute focus groups in which clergy voluntarily shared their stories of loneliness and social isolation, as well as what helps them feel more connected. We further completed an extensive literature review of current research to help better understand the extent of loneliness in our society. Finally, we (Mary Kay and Mark) have been fortunate to cofacilitate a fifteen-month clergy loneliness and belonging group in which we have heard firsthand the challenges and blessings of ministry when it comes to friendships, family relationships, and congregational interactions.

In this book, you will find a lot of stories. All the stories you will read are real. The identities and specifics of individuals in the stories, however, are changed to protect each person's privacy. In our work, confidentiality is a core value, and we've intentionally written these stories with that sacred trust in mind.

Additionally, many of the stories and our words have a Christian bent. This is simply because our work is primarily with Christian faith communities. If you are a clergyperson of another faith tradition, we are delighted you are reading this book, and it is for you too.

Acknowledgments

As always, a book project is never the work of only the authors. We'd like to thank all our LeaderWise colleagues for their thoughtful conversations, advice, and support, and especially Drs. Dan Nelson and Danny Elenz for bringing their gifts to the project. Dan created, administered, and analyzed the original research on loneliness at LeaderWise. Danny provided an extensive literature review and conducted focus groups in support of our work. Without their help, the book would not have been possible.

We are forever grateful for the loneliness and belonging support group with whom we've been journeying for over a year. We have learned so much from this group of pastors, and we feel a deep connection with each of them.

Indelible gratitude goes to Dr. Patricia McCarthy Veach, our writing coach, and Rev. Dr. Beth Gaede, our editor at 1517 Media. Their constant guidance, encouragement, and belief in the project kept us going. Our manuscript improved every time they brought their gifts to it.

Finally, we thank our spouses for the grace they've shown for the extra hours spent on writing these pages, and for our quirky profession in general!

Introduction

Over two hundred years ago, communities in America were built around a town center of some sort—the park, the town hall, and undoubtedly the church. Large homes with front porches bordered these common spaces, which contributed to a community's ability to build relationships together. Children played while parents chatted about life, and they shared meals on green spaces under the canopy and comfort of massive oaks and maples. Visit a small town today, and you can see remnants of this idyllic time.

I (Mary Kay) have an obsession with front porches. Drive me down any street and ask me which house is my favorite. Undoubtedly, it will be the one with the largest front porch. Walking around the city where I live, I gaze at front porches and imagine how people live on them. I look for cozy sitting spaces and dining tables. I am drawn to porches occupied by people connecting with one another. The front porch, an architectural mainstay in the nineteenth and early twentieth centuries, was a focal point for building relationships. Porches were a place to stop and say hi to your neighbor, talk about life, and beat the heat because "air-conditioning" was a breeze any way you could get it.

There's something nostalgic about the front porch. The big house my husband and I built together while our kids were growing up had a large front porch, and I spent a bit of every day on it. The small, 120-year-old bungalow in the city where we now live has a generous (compared to the size of the house) front porch. We sit in comfortable chairs, eat our meals there, share wine with friends. From my front porch, I am able to carry on conversations with neighbors and unknown passersby, who are walking their dogs or following their kids on the way down to the park at the end of the street. We talk about gardens, the weather, dogs, kids, and the complicated times in which we live. Even the most basic contact reminds me that we are beings designed for connection, and it can happen with the simplicity of a smile, the meeting of the eyes, the wave of a hand, or a brief conversation.

A writer from the University of Virginia observes, "Between the rise of the front porch in the middle nineteenth century and its decline in the post-World War II era, the front porch developed a cultural significance. It represented the cultural ideals of family, community, and nature. As these ideals would decline in importance in American culture, so would the porch."[1] "Car culture" and air-conditioning changed our lives and society. As cars made it possible to go farther faster, people made their homes in suburbia, and air-conditioning gave families relief from the heat. People began spending more time inside—inside their homes, their cars, their offices. Front porches largely became a thing of the past, along with civic engagement of all kinds. As the front porches of American family homes have dwindled, so too has loneliness increased. We've taken our lives inside, literally and figuratively, to a lonelier place.

For a few years now, researchers have been studying the rise of loneliness. We'll explore some of those statistics in chapters 2 and 3. Vivek Murthy was the surgeon general during the Obama administration and, at the time of this writing, the Biden administration. At the outset of his first tenure, he took to the streets of America and listened to the needs of the people. Across America, Murthy was surprised to notice that "loneliness ran like a dark thread through many of the more obvious issues that people brought to my attention, like addiction, violence, anxiety, and depression."[2] Murthy was so concerned about pervasive loneliness that he called it an epidemic.

Perhaps contributing to the loneliness epidemic, the cultural values of rugged individualism and self-determinism in the United States seem to produce shame when we think we don't measure up to the standards set by society. Whether we feel shame because we're addicted, we're overweight, we have a mental health diagnosis, or we have experienced sexual violence—whether we have been through divorce, or have never found a spouse, or have felt oppressed due to our sexual or racial identity, we can feel shamed by a society that says we each have the ability to achieve whatever we desire if we just pick ourselves up by our bootstraps. Shame causes us to isolate, to go inward. We become lonely.

Loneliness isn't just borne out of shame, however. The busyness of our lives and the culture of overwork cause us to give up many things, such as important relationships, because of a need and desire to achieve more. Busyness, too, can begin a cycle of feeling cut off from those people who are important to us and the communal activities that keep us connected.

In Murthy's tour across America, he also saw the healing power of human connection when community building is intentional. When people gather to experience life together, to attend to a social justice or societal need together, human connection is the balm that soothes the wounds of loneliness. This "seesaw relationship between loneliness and togetherness"[3] impelled Murthy to use his platform to raise awareness about the epidemic of loneliness in the United States. In his book *Together: The Healing Power of Human Connection in a Sometimes Lonely World*, Murthy documents how social connection facilitates healing, wholeness, and well-being.

Across my adult life, I (Mark) have experienced the benefits of social connection with a group of ten college friends. We attended a small liberal arts college, where we honed our values and life perspectives through our studies, conversations, and shared activities, and continued our exploration of life together after graduation. We gathered frequently as young professionals. Then as parents of young children, we together shepherded them from infancy to adulthood.

At some point, several in our group started to refer to ourselves as "the Village," even though we lived in different communities. The name stuck. For me, though, the full weight and meaning of that term became apparent only upon the death of my father. Through his final week of life, my family gathered around him at the hospital, and the Village texted and called frequently. My wife, who is also part of the Village, and I felt very supported. And then, completely unexpected, the entire Village showed up at my father's funeral, which involved a trip of two to three hours for almost all of them. As they trickled in prior to the service, I felt buoyed in my grief. Though it was one of the saddest days of my life, as I loved my father deeply, I felt surrounded and held by the love of friends. The Village was there for me, and I experienced an almost ethereal peace and assurance to realize they would journey with me the rest of my life too. When my time comes, I have no doubt that the Village will surround me once again. The balm of social connection was made evident to me that day.

Murthy talks about a phenomenon similar to my Village on the island of Okinawa, though it dates back centuries. It has been tradition for parents of young children to gather together to establish a "moai," a group who journeys through life together. Parents make a point of meeting at least weekly and sometimes even daily (their children are included in the gathering), and this practice continues for the children for the rest of their lives. Through all the joys and vicissitudes of life, the moai supports one another. As Murthy describes it,

"A moai is like a second family," adding that people in a moai share a common purpose of "companionship and advice" across their life spans.[4] In contemporary times, a moai can be formed at any point during one's life, and the practice continues to thrive in Okinawa.

As our physical, cultural, and social environments change, certain avenues for connection are disappearing—for instance, front porches. Opportunities for spontaneous connection are less frequent. Social connection requires greater intentionality. Whether we are part of a village or a moai, the point is that meaningful social connections can be formed intentionally. Murthy, after reading about moais, decided to form his own. He describes feeling adrift when he was new to a community, raising young children, and feeling lonely. At a retreat, he met people at about the same stage of life who had similar challenges, and he asked if they would like to form a virtual moai that would meet once a month for two hours or more. Together they shared their lives and supported one another through difficult times. He observes that connecting regularly moved them from "having friendship" to "experiencing friendship" to arriving at a point of deep personal connection. He concludes, "Instead of relying on fate or impulse to bring us together, we made an explicit commitment to be there for each other. The moai structure enabled us to act on that commitment. It minimized the risk that inertia would let us drift apart."[5]

In a focus group, pastor Amelia shared with us her struggle with what she named as a three-year cycle of loneliness due to frequent moves during her life: "My husband and I have moved five times together, due to his job. It takes so long to develop deep friendships. I try not to make friends in the church, but then I have no time outside of church. In my last congregation, I was working fifty to sixty hours, and I'd go home and think, 'How *can* I make friends?' How do I have time when I'm trying to be a mother and a (more than) full-time pastor at the same time? I'm very aware of how exhausting it's been."

Pastor Dan shared simply, "In seven years, I have never been invited into a member's home for a meal and a visit. I've been there for pastoral care, but never for anything other than my pastoral role."

These are common stories from the lived experiences of clergy in the United States. Harvard University studied loneliness in a variety of professions. They found that employees in extremely social, people-oriented roles such as social work, marketing, and sales were the least likely to be lonely.[6] So one would think pastors have it made. We have a built-in community! Sadly, it isn't true. Pastors are just as lonely as the rest of the population, and in one particular way, they are lonelier than the rest of the population, which we'll talk about in the coming pages.

Brené Brown talks about what it means to belong and says that one of three possibilities happens when one doesn't feel like they belong in their family: (1) we live in pain and seek to numb it; (2) we deny the pain and pass it on; or (3) we find the courage to own the pain, develop empathy for ourselves and others, and begin to name similar hurt in the world.[7] This book isn't explicitly talking about feelings of not belonging in families, but we believe the same dynamic holds true for pastors who feel like they don't belong in the systems in which they find themselves. *And* we believe that pastors who are able to own their pain, starting from the place of claiming their feelings of loneliness, will not only improve their own well-being but also have a unique opportunity to help heal the hurts of the world.

Our intentions in writing this book are to name the epidemic of loneliness that we have seen in our work with clergy; to normalize and reframe it for you and with you, dear reader; and to explore ways to overcome the loneliness present in ministry. If we can start with ourselves and change the state of connection for clergy, then perhaps we can also begin to change how our faith communities perceive their role by being social connectors in their own neighborhoods, thereby beginning to solve the epidemic of loneliness in the United States. But make no mistake, our primary aim is to address the pervasive sense of loneliness we have come to see present in ministry.

As we noted earlier, the stories in this book are real. We believe the stories bring the dimensions of clergy loneliness into full focus, and we use the stories to illustrate the empirical research and psychological models of loneliness, which is a lived experience. Given the nature of our work in counseling and consulting, we've also gone to great lengths to protect the identities and privacy of individuals by using the types of stories we've heard over and over again from ministers, as well as changing any identifying details and creating fictionalized names.

The book is divided into three parts. In part 1, we talk about the epidemic of loneliness in general, and with clergy specifically. In part 2, we explore the paths back to belonging.

Each chapter in the book begins with a case scenario and invites you to think a bit about how you relate to the situation described therein. Then the chapter offers research findings, tools, and strategies. At the end of each chapter, we offer some questions for reflection and discussion. *Our invitation to you is this: consider inviting a small group of trusted colleagues to read this book with you, and use the questions at the end of each chapter for discussion. This act, in and of itself, will reduce feelings of loneliness!*

It is in our (Mark and Mary Kay) nature to look for and point to hope. In part 3, we propose to judicatories and congregations how they can do their part. In addition to suggesting how they can support their clergy, we return to the topic of societal loneliness and consider how congregations might be the center of a shift in our culture toward social connectedness. In the church, we worry a lot about church decline, but the truth is, church decline coincides with the decline of other means of civic engagement, "from voter turnout to bridge clubs, from volunteer fire departments to marching bands, from alumni organizations to bowling leagues."[8] With the ways in which we historically experienced social connection going by the wayside, it is increasingly important for us to find new ways to connect. The point is, loneliness is an epidemic in part because those ways of connecting that people historically relied on, including church, are mostly gone or declining. Pastors, too, need to find new ways of connecting so that they can combat the loneliness within their roles and lives. And as a bonus, what if the church found a *new* way (or maybe resurrected an old way!) to be that social connection again, as it perhaps once was almost a century ago? We will wonder about that at the end of the book.

PART I

The Epidemic of Loneliness

We aren't the first people to write about loneliness. It has already been named an epidemic, and that was before the Covid-19 pandemic sent people into their houses for months on end. Clergy are just as lonely as the general population and more so in one particular way.

In part 1 of this book, we explore what loneliness is and reflect on the current state of loneliness and isolation in the United States. We then discuss the particular plight of clergy. The message to clergy here is that you aren't alone. There is nothing wrong with you. The fact is, the unique role clergy hold tends to isolate us. Please know there is hope—that comes in part 2 of the book.

1

What Is Loneliness?

Loneliness is like an iceberg—it goes deeper than we can see.

—John T. Cacioppo, *Loneliness*

But Ruth said, "Do not press me to leave you or to turn back from following you! Where you go, I will go; where you lodge, I will lodge; your people shall be my people, and your God my God."

—Ruth 1:16

Judy was a middle-aged second-career pastor who answered her call to ministry after fifteen years in a fast-paced, rough-and-tumble corporate environment. In addition to the relief of finally saying yes to ministry, which she rightly perceived would give her a greater sense of day-to-day meaning as she finally lived into the call she had sensed for so long, Judy

*looked forward to establishing deep, emotionally rich rela-
tionships with her parishioners. And in one sense, she did
experience that. She was invited into the sacred moments of
parishioners' lives, including births, marriages, and deaths. On
the other hand, though, she was surprised to find herself
on the outside looking in—something she hadn't thought
about experiencing as she began the process of becoming a
pastor. As much as she wanted to be part of their inner circle
of friends and family, she was "pastor," and clergy tended to
stay, on average, about three years in this small community.
People welcomed clergy but kept them at arm's length when
it came to casual socializing. As a result, Judy was surprised
to discover how lonely ministry actually felt in comparison to
the corporate world.*

FOR REFLECTION

- To what parts of Judy's story do you relate?
- When you began ministry, what were your
  expectations about being in relationship with
  parishioners? With the community?

We humans have an intense, innate need for social connection. It is actually wired into us as part of our survival strategy.
Historically, tribes were communities formed for the protec-
tion of the whole and the propagation of the species. Without
others, our ancient ancestors would literally have perished as
a species. When one became separated from the tribe, they

would be in potential danger. So natural selection developed a biological response to that disconnection that today we call loneliness.

Clergy have a built-in community through our congregations, a network of people through which to make friends. But just because we are in a helping profession and have a built-in network doesn't mean we aren't lonely. In our (Mary Kay's and Mark's) work with clergy, we've discovered that ministry can be a very lonely profession.

As clergy, many of us have encountered the dynamic of being lonely while in the company of others. Like Judy in the opening story experienced, we find loneliness can feel more intense if we are with a group of people but kept on the margins for friendship and socializing. On the one hand, we are "set apart" for the work of ministry, as we're called to live our lives differently than most, "to be in the world but not of this world." On the other hand, this aspect of our calling can contribute to a profound experience of being cut off or left out. Friendship is one-sided, if it is present at all, as we can never fully share our most vulnerable selves with congregation members.

If we are experiencing emotional pain, we may also choose to self-isolate to protect ourselves, which can further fuel our loneliness. When I (Mary Kay) was going through a divorce, colleagues knew that when I didn't have my children, they could find me in my office late at night working. I didn't want to be alone in my house, and throwing myself into my work was a perfect distraction, but I also felt shame around the divorce and didn't want to talk about it with others. It was a very lonely time. A colleague and friend, who was single too, came in late one night and, during our conversation, said, "I'd rather be lonely and alone than lonely and with someone." It gave me pause, then I had to agree.

As suggested previously, at its core, loneliness is a biological signal to find deeper connection. John Cacioppo, a pioneering researcher in the psychology of loneliness, conceptualized it as akin to hunger pangs or yawns.[1] Our stomachs growl; we find food. We yawn, and we recognize that we're tired and seek rest. Our feelings of loneliness are meant to be a signal too. When we're lonely, our evolutionary past is telling us to proactively seek out social connection within our tribe for both our physical (safety) and our mental health.

While this important biological signal was a life-or-death reaction for our ancestors who became separated from their tribe, loneliness continues to function as a stress response. When we're lonely, our bodies release an abundance of hormones, such as epinephrine, to cause our systems to go on high alert. The endocrine system is activated and releases cortisol, which increases blood pressure and releases blood sugars. Like most stress responses, however, it's helpful in small doses but can become problematic when chronic. While life-preserving in an emergency, this anxiety-producing systemic response is not sustainable for the long term, such as in cases of chronic loneliness. Over time, overfunctioning systems induce cardiovascular stress and inflammation, damaging tissues and blood vessels and increasing the risk of heart disease and other chronic illnesses. What's more, this bodily response causes poor sleep patterns, which in and of itself is a physical and mental health risk factor.

When we feel the pangs of loneliness and our biological systems kick in, our bodies have a couple natural responses. The first is to seek out social support—to reconnect with the tribe. But interestingly, many of us do the opposite and withdraw when our stress is related to loneliness.

Another natural response is to go on high alert; that is, we misread other people's behavior and interpret it negatively. We begin to misread social situations, telling ourselves stories that may be incorrect. When friends haven't called, we think, "They don't like me." When we walk into a party feeling awkward, we don't know where to turn or who to talk to, so instead of reaching out for the social connection we need, we withdraw. This self-critical thinking causes us to withdraw further, which can accelerate into a downward spiral, resulting in even greater withdrawal and loneliness.[2]

We humans have this intense need for social connection, and like an immune system that rejects an artificial organ, the biological response of loneliness can backfire on us. We withdraw rather than reach out because we've misinterpreted the situation. Making assumptions about what other people are thinking never does us any good, and comparing our social situation to others' also does us no favors because we each have a different level of need for social connection.

GENETIC PREDISPOSITION AND
SOCIAL CONNECTION

We have all had conversations debating nature versus nurture on everyday topics like "Why is my child good at running?" or more abstract questions like "Are leaders born or made?" The answer in a lot of debates is "Yes!" There is almost always a both/and explanation. The same is true with respect to our desire for social connection.

A genetic component appears to underlie our desire for relationships, and scientists are beginning to identify specific genes that determine our set point for sociability. As we know from our daily experiences in ministry and in our personal lives, some people desire more social interactions and others want fewer. We all know people who from infancy and early childhood were either more or less socially inclined. Biological predisposition likely plays a role in our desire for social interaction, and yet when our interactions fail to rise to the level of our biological need, our susceptibility to loneliness increases. This predisposition is not the same as when we, as ministers, talk about our preference for introversion versus extraversion. I (Mary Kay) am an introvert, and yet I deeply need social connection. The way I meet that need may look different from the way my extroverted friends do, but the need is there.

Similar to other characteristics, though, loneliness involves more than biology. So we propose *a social connection formula*, which in addition to genetics includes culture (our environment) and social cognition (our interpretation of our social situation). The formula is

$$\text{genetic predisposition} + \text{culture} + \text{social cognition} = \text{our experience of belonging/loneliness}$$

This formula explains both satisfaction with relationships as well as our feelings of loneliness when relationships are lacking.

Consider, for example, Joe, a youth minister who grew up with numerous friends in his hometown and found more friends in college. At age thirty-three, he was serving in a small town in Texas and felt isolated. He had felt passionate about youth ministry for the first several years, and he enjoyed coming to know almost everyone in his rural community. We are enculturated to believe what "normal" social connection looks like, however, and now Joe had begun to experience some stirrings of loneliness. Friends and siblings were starting to marry, and people were asking if he was serious about anyone. These events only reminded him of how lonely he felt. Joe confessed, "I want to be with someone—and with all my friends and siblings getting married, I'm worried that my chance has passed me by."

The social connection formula helps us understand Joe's loneliness. His lifelong enjoyment of people would point to a genetic predisposition of a deeper need for connection, and his environment, or culture, is telling him it would be developmentally appropriate—in fact, expected—that he be "serious" about someone at his age. Joe's thoughts, or social cognition, tell him to be on high alert, as his opportunity for a committed, intimate relationship might unwittingly pass him by. All of these factors together have contributed to his deepening loneliness.

THE CULTURE CONNECTION

Rugged individualism is a core value we have seen at work since the founding of our country. Many people emigrated from Europe seeking to escape the limitations of the "Old World" and to pursue the opportunities of the "New World." Coming to this continent, some of which later became the United States, held the promise of a metaphorical release from bondage for people who felt oppressed or marginalized, and the myth of anyone being able to make their own way if they just work hard enough was born, as was a system of meritocracy. Alexis de Tocqueville was a Frenchman who toured the United States in the early 1800s and wrote a classic work on the American character called *Democracy in America*.[3] He was impressed by the centrality of rugged individualism in the American psyche. Rather prophetically, however, he warned that individualism needs a strong counterbalance of community-oriented values and habits, or else American society would experience fragmentation and social isolation.

In some ways, the founding American value of rugged individualism is a failed experiment. *Every person for themselves* has led to a culture of life as a zero-sum game, resulting in competition, power grabs, and a lack of compassion for one's neighbors as well as the *least of these*. Sure, we each need to grow up to become individuated from those around us. That is what it means to develop one's identity. However, we cannot be individuals outside of relationship. And regardless of your faith tradition, being in relationship—relationship with self, relationship with God, and relationship with our neighbors—is core to our spiritual journey. It appears the American value of rugged individualism, true to de Tocqueville's prediction, has indeed fragmented and isolated us.

We have witnessed firsthand the deleterious impact of rugged individualism on people in ministry. In a focus group of male-identifying clergy, a pastor named Robert remarked, "Seventy-five percent of the time I feel completely ill-equipped for ministry." Around the table, clergy nodded. Despite statistics documenting that the decline of churches in the United States is widespread, Robert had taken on the full weight of responsibility for his congregation's drop in worship attendance, membership, and financial resources. Although Robert was surrounded by other pastors in the room who had similar struggles, he felt isolated and alone, as if his situation were unique. He had bought into the cultural myth of rugged individualism and thought that through his own effort and self-reliance, his ministry and church would be the exception to the rule. It was crushing for him to discover this was not so—and he blamed himself. Thankfully, as Robert vulnerably shared his experience, he relaxed, relief spread across his face, and all of those years of self-judgment began to ease. Robert gave the group a gift, as other pastors also started to let down their guards. Together they moved from individualism and isolation to sharing, connection, and mutual support.

Robert's self-disclosure is remarkable given the cultural norm, especially for people who identify as male, to hide vulnerability both from themselves and others. According to Brené Brown, we live in a culture that tells us being vulnerable and tender shows weakness, for which our culture has little tolerance. In an interview with Work of the People, Brown suggests we have lost the capacity to hold space for pain and discomfort and suggests that the loss is due to an *inability* to sit with unpleasant feelings. We literally don't know how to do that.[4]

In our work with clergy, we see this inability to sit in pain and discomfort play out with loneliness. Because loneliness has become stigmatized, we attach shame to it. And due to our shame, which is often beneath the surface of our loneliness, we avoid (or hide from others, and sometimes even from ourselves) our vulnerability and feelings of loneliness rather than acknowledge them. As we have learned from our work with clergy, which Robert also discovered, the best way to deal with self-judgment, shame, and loneliness is to acknowledge one's experience forthrightly and reach out to others for support. We'll talk about social support later in the book.

SOCIAL COGNITION: BRINGING IT ALL TOGETHER

The final variable in the social connection formula further explains our experience of loneliness and offers a path forward to manage it. The *cognitive discrepancy model* of loneliness presupposes the factors of genetic predisposition and cultural influences and then suggests our loneliness is often precipitated by a social experience or event that goes poorly.[5] Reflecting upon this event, we unconsciously assess the degree of alignment between our desired relationships and our actual experience of them. If we subconsciously perceive a mismatch, we interpret and make attributions about it. Those of us who are prone to loneliness will often make a negative attribution, as loneliness colors our view of ourselves and our relationships. For instance, if we feel lonely and attend a social event, we are likely to assume the worst if we perceive that few people are talking to us. We might say to ourselves things like "I knew it. Nobody likes me here," "Just confirms it—these people are so unfriendly," or "I'll never have any friends." We then feel even lonelier and might consequently experience greater self-judgment and isolation. The cognitive discrepancy model is one of the most widely validated models for how loneliness works. Figure 1.1 illustrates the components.

The good news is, this model also offers a path forward to manage loneliness and gain a greater sense of belonging. For instance, while some of us may have a greater genetic predisposition to loneliness, and we all hear cultural messages about rugged individualism and vulnerability, we can learn to adjust our thinking and interpretations to a more optimistic frame—still realistic yet hopeful. The last step of the model, "reactions and coping," offers room for other strategies, such as developing and nurturing friendships as a clergyperson, practicing self-soothing strategies during times of

Predisposing Factors
- Personality
- Culture

$+$

Precipitating Events

$\downarrow$

Desired Social Relations

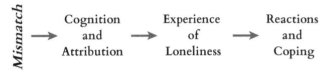

Actual Social Relations

Figure 1.1. Cognitive discrepancy model

loneliness, and transforming loneliness into solitude. We will explore these practices in subsequent chapters. First, however, although loneliness is a part of the human condition, we will explore how clergy stand out from the general population.

FOR REFLECTION AND DISCUSSION

1. We all have a biological need for social connection. Given what you've read, how would you describe your need for social connection compared to some other people you know?

2. What messages in our cultural society have been given to you about social connection?

3. How, if at all, has your need for social connection changed over time? Why do you think that is?

2

The Impact of Loneliness

Loneliness is different than isolation and solitude. Loneliness is a subjective feeling where the connections we need are greater than the connections we have. In the gap, we experience loneliness.

—Vivek Murthy, *Together*

Gaylord lived up the stairs and to the right in our (Mark and spouse's) run-down apartment building. As a newly married couple in our midtwenties, and with me being in graduate school, we had little money. We moved into the best apartment we could afford, which wasn't much. Gaylord, in his late fifties and with multiple chronic health concerns, likely moved into the best apartment he could afford too. Although he was a professor at the local university, he did unsteady contract work, and his finances appeared to be precarious. He also was wrestling with the emotional effects of a contentious divorce, estrangement from his children, and serious health issues. The combination had taken its toll, worn down his spirit, and isolated him. When we invited him to church one Sunday, he leaped at the chance. The congregation warmly welcomed him—and yet the losses in his life were so great that his loneliness was palpable. I have often wondered about the chicken-or-egg phenomenon—which came first, his profound loneliness or his chronic health concerns? Or did they somehow occur in tandem?

FOR REFLECTION

- To what part of this story do you relate?
- Thinking through the seasons of your life, when have you felt loneliest?

THE MIND-BODY CONNECTION

Have you ever had a stress headache at work or felt sick to your stomach about a strained relationship? There is no doubt that the mind and body are one and what affects us emotionally affects us physically too. The science of loneliness demonstrates that the same is true for loneliness, and in our counseling and consulting work, we have come to think of loneliness as "embodied," as it impacts the whole person.

Almost twenty years ago, researchers created a mock video game in which participants thought they were playing with two other people, passing a ball back and forth—and then they were unexpectedly excluded. Their real-time brain scans showed that the emotions accompanying this act of social exclusion lit up the same circuits as physical pain.[1] Another study found a similar result: emotional pain was experienced as physical pain in the brain when researchers flashed recently jilted lovers' pictures of their exes.[2] On a happier note, a third group of researchers found that acetaminophen, or Tylenol, actually took the edge off emotional pain for participants who had recently suffered a broken heart.[3] Recently, using meta-analysis (a statistical procedure that analyzes the results of several previous studies), researchers have called into question whether emotional and physical pain are the same. In fact, the pain of social rejection was found to be far more complex—involving more aspects of the brain, as it consistently pulled in circuitry related to relationships and memory too.[4] People still feel loneliness as pain but perhaps in a more profound way than a stubbed toe.

The long-term physical toll of loneliness is real too. We now have decades worth of data that show people who are lonely are at greater risk of premature death—on average about a 26 percent increase.[5] Although we often associate the harmful effects of loneliness with older adults, recent research has found there is a much stronger causal relationship between loneliness and mortality for those in their middle years than for any other age group.[6] Loneliness also takes its largest toll on middle-aged adults—again more than any other age group—in contributing to day-to-day health problems, both physical and emotional. One hypothesis is that middle-aged (and younger) people may experience the health effects of loneliness more acutely than older adults because it's less expected. Many of us, rightly or wrongly, picture older people as lonely and isolated, sitting by themselves on evenings or weekends, while we assume younger people should have a more active social life. Consequently, younger people may feel lonelier when friends or family don't call, which further fuels emotional pain and physical consequences, ultimately contributing to premature death.

One way to make sense of these findings is to compare them to other physical health risks. In estimating the risk of premature death from different causes, one set of researchers has noted the following increases in probability: 5 percent if you live in an area with heavy air pollution, 20 percent if you are obese, 30 percent if you regularly abuse alcohol, and 45 percent if you live with chronic loneliness. In fact, the researchers concluded the risk of premature death due to persistent loneliness is equivalent to the risk from smoking fifteen cigarettes per day![7]

Social science researchers have long thought that the risk of loneliness depends on your *perception* of your social network, specifically whether you are satisfied with it rather than the actual number of individuals in it. If you have a few social contacts with whom you feel connected, even if another person has many, you may not feel lonely or suffer the consequences of loneliness. Some recent research is now calling that belief into question. Findings suggest that three factors—social isolation (a measure of the objective number of people in one's social network), loneliness (a measure of the subjective perception of being satisfied with one's social network), and living alone—are fairly equally predictive of emotional and physical health concerns, including premature death.[8]

For clergy, these findings are noteworthy. For example, our research has shown that clergy have about the same level of loneliness as the general population but a higher rate of social isolation due to their role, as they are set apart from congregation members and geographically separated from their families.[9] According to the broader research, this could place clergy at significant risk for emotional and physical health issues.

It is important to note, however, that statistical probability does not have to predict destiny. We share these findings to raise your awareness so you can take proactive measures to address possible risk factors. If you live alone, for instance, you might be more intentional about setting aside time to reach out to family and friends via social media and technology or, even better, scheduling regular in-person visits throughout the year. We include a number of additional ideas later in this book to address the challenges of loneliness and social isolation.

Tyrone grew up in Baltimore amid a rich network of family and friends. After a brief career as a political operative in

Washington, DC, he discerned a call to ministry, attended seminary, and accepted his first call—to rural North Carolina. Tyrone had always lived in urban settings and anticipated a bit of culture shock in this move. As he considered relocation, he made sure there was a regional airport within an hour's drive and negotiated a call package that would offer enough financial resources and time for a trip home to see family and friends annually or, ideally, every six months. At the same time, Tyrone was realistic and knew that finances would be tight as a pastor. Yet he remarked about the trips home, "This is a nonnegotiable. These are the people I'm walking through life with."

THE EPIDEMIC OF LONELINESS

The deleterious emotional and physical impact of loneliness might be of less concern to us if loneliness were an unusual, infrequent condition. The evidence, though, shows that loneliness has reached epidemic proportions among the general public. Some of the most interesting research on the prevalence of loneliness in the United States has been conducted by Cigna, a prominent health insurance company, in two large studies completed in 2018 and 2020.[10] The fact that an insurance company would expend financial resources on loneliness research speaks to its importance for emotional and physical health, as they have a vested interest in our staying healthy. Their findings are startling. Here is a selection of their most concerning findings:

- In 2018, 54 percent of us felt lonely, and by 2019, this number had increased to 61 percent.
- Loneliness varied by generation and decreased with age; 79 percent of Generation Z, 71 percent of millennials, and 50 percent of baby boomers reported feeling lonely.
- Forty-three percent of us said we are socially isolated.
- Forty-three percent described our relationships as not being meaningful.
- Twenty-seven percent believed that others rarely or never understand us.
- One in five of us felt like we have no one in whom we can confide.

Because clergy are part of the general population, it is reasonable to conclude that they are not immune to the widespread experience of loneliness. Our research at LeaderWise bears this out. In 2019, we conducted a national survey of over five hundred clergy across denominations, using the same well-validated loneliness scale (UCLA Loneliness Scale [Version 3]) as the Cigna studies. The central finding is that clergy loneliness scores are on average the same as those of the general population. As the general population suffers, so do we.[11]

Based on our day-to-day observations and experiences, many of us will have some guesses about factors that might predict clergy loneliness, such as living in a rural setting, being single, or serving as a woman in ministry. These are all legitimate guesses, and we know many clergy in these different life circumstances who are lonely. Our research, though, looked at these and other factors from a more global perspective, and our results support some of these assumptions and challenge others. Specifically, we found five variables that do *not* predict clergy loneliness: age, years in ministry, identifying as male or female, identifying with a race or ethnicity, and geographic location. We also found four variables that were most predictive of clergy loneliness: living apart from one's partner, not being in a relationship, having a disability, and belonging to a denomination that has a congregational focus (e.g., United Church of Christ, Unitarian Universalist) rather than a connectional emphasis (e.g., United Methodist). Our research further suggests the *way* in which clergy experience loneliness may be different from the general population.

Ongoing statistical research of the UCLA loneliness survey has demonstrated that there are three main factors, or distinct components, of loneliness measured by the inventory. According to researchers, the factors are (1) individual isolation, in which we feel different from those around us, separated emotionally and socially from others, and alone; (2) relational loneliness, in which we view ourselves as lacking a social network of support; and (3) collective loneliness, in which we are missing out on meaningful group affiliations, such as with our professional organizations, civic clubs, faith communities, and the like.[12]

Our LeaderWise study shows that the driving factor behind clergy loneliness is individual isolation. Our scores for feeling connected to friends and family (relational component of loneliness) and finding purpose by belonging to a larger whole (collective component of loneliness) are the same as for the general population, but we suffer most acutely from a sense of feeling left out, excluded, and sometimes rejected (isolation component of loneliness). Poignantly, the ten statements about loneliness that clergy in our study endorsed most strongly relate to social isolation. In short, we feel different from those around us—the people among whom we live and with whom we interact every day. Consider the following:

- Over 60 percent of clergy endorsed "sometimes" or "always" the items "You feel like you lack companionship" and "People are around you but not with you."
- Over 55 percent of clergy endorsed "sometimes" or "always" the items "You feel left out," "You feel that your interests and ideas are not shared by those around you," and "You feel isolated from others."
- Over half of clergy endorsed "sometimes" or "always" the items "You feel alone" and "You feel that no one really knows you well."[13]

Whether the Covid-19 pandemic affected the rates of loneliness and isolation is a fair question. In fact, Julianne Holt-Lunstad, one of the foremost researchers on loneliness, sounded the alarm in June 2020. Writing in *Health Affairs*, she noted that 28 percent of the American population lives alone, and for these individuals the pandemic was especially difficult because they had no physical contact. Citing several studies, she further observed that loneliness had increased 20 to 30 percent in a three-month period, and emotional distress had tripled.[14]

Although we lack specific research on the impact of the pandemic on clergy loneliness, we can speculate that it might be similar given how closely the clergy rate of loneliness tracks with the general population. In addition, with the onset of the pandemic, clergy frequently shared with us their dismay at no longer being able to perform their most basic ministerial functions (e.g., pastoral visits, in-person worship leadership, weddings, funerals). These functions in the past often provided great vocational satisfaction and made up for—to some degree—the sacrifice of being set apart and feeling different from others. During the pandemic, many pastors mostly felt at loose ends vocationally, socially isolated, and alone.

THE HEALING BALM OF SOCIAL CONNECTION

Viewed through a lens of loneliness, the effects of social isolation—increased rates of morbidity and mortality—look dire for both clergy and the general population. On a brighter note, though, we can choose a different lens, looking at the healing impact of social support and connectedness.

In 2010, Julianne Holt-Lunstad and colleagues conducted a meta-analysis of the results of 148 studies on belonging, loneliness, morbidity, and mortality involving a total of more than three hundred thousand participants. They concluded that being socially connected—having a sense of belonging—increased the odds of survival by 50 percent for any given period of time. This effect became even stronger when a person was considered socially integrated into their community—that is, when they were actively engaged in relationships, identified with the larger community, and held meaningful social roles. When these factors were in place, the chances of survival increased to 91 percent.[15] A 2015 follow-up meta-analysis by this team of researchers included over three million participants and confirmed these results. They concluded that social connectedness and belonging may well be the path for counteracting the ill effects of loneliness and social isolation.[16]

After taking a deeper look at the factors that contribute to the experience of loneliness among clergy, we'll turn our attention in part 2 to some of the balms we've identified, especially for clergy, that take us down the path toward belonging.

FOR REFLECTION AND DISCUSSION

1. We offered many reasons people feel lonely. Considering times in your life when you've felt lonely, were any of these the cause, or was the feeling about something else?

2. At times when you've felt lonely or isolated, what has been the impact on your whole person (physically, emotionally, spiritually, etc.)?

3. Of the variables that are predictive for loneliness, which ones are true for you *now* in your life? What is their impact?

3

The Clergy Life

Lots of people lean on me. Who do I get to lean on?

—Focus group participant

In a virtual counseling session during the early days of the pandemic, Emily shared her story. She began, "I knew my marriage needed some work, but when Covid hit, it became clear it wasn't going to survive. All of a sudden, I didn't know where to turn. I couldn't share about my relationship with my congregation, and I didn't get any support from my judicatory. Colleagues who I thought were friends stopped calling, I suppose because they didn't know what to say. After I finally told the congregation, via letter, compassionate members reached out to see how I was doing, but I can't share deeply with them. I am always putting on a brave face. I feel like I have nowhere to turn."

Emily had been serving her congregation for about five years, and like so many people in ministry, she found her work to be all-consuming. Additionally, she was hundreds of miles from the place she called home and hadn't made friends in her current community. She had no one locally outside her marriage with whom she felt she had an intimate relationship. Prior to the pandemic, she didn't want to admit to herself that there were issues in her marriage, so she just worked harder and longer, telling herself she'd deal with her personal issues "tomorrow." Tomorrows turned into months and years, and soon she was facing the isolation and loneliness of a divorce. She had reached out to the judicatory staff that she expected to support her, and when she shared with them that she was headed for divorce, she felt nothing from them but a cold shoulder, which led her to feel deep shame. She didn't reach out to them again, and she began to fear that if she didn't pull herself together, her ministry would also be in jeopardy. She felt like she was in a downward spiral.

FOR REFLECTION

- To what parts of Emily's story do you relate?
- Who can provide you with deep support for those hardest times in life?

Clergy have unique relationships with their parishioners. We immerse ourselves fully in the lives of those in our congregations and communities as we live our own lives amid theirs, and yet we must keep them, to some degree, at arm's length due to the professional ethics of our role. In the case scenario that opened this chapter, Emily felt both supported by her congregation and unable to share the depth of her distress with them. This tension—to be simultaneously dedicated to and immersed in our communities, which can often bring great joy, and yet not be fully known by them—is inherent in the clergy life. Ultimately, this can contribute to our experience of isolation.

In addition, we have observed several other factors that often fuel clergy isolation and loneliness:

- Unrealistic expectations. Expectations are high for clergy, not only from the people in the pews, but also from clergy themselves.
- Going where the calls are. Clergy move around a lot to go where we are called, often to places where we would not typically choose to live.
- The need to maintain boundaries. From seminary on, we are encouraged to keep firm boundaries around our relationships, which can hinder building deep relationships.
- Inability to be authentic. We feel we have few safe spaces in which to be truly vulnerable and authentic.
- Theological and ideological differences. Many times, clergy have a different understanding of the world from their parishioners'.

As we began to discuss in chapter 2, LeaderWise has done our own research on clergy loneliness. In this chapter, we will delve into these factors that contribute to the unique sense of loneliness clergy can feel. At the end of the chapter, we reflect briefly on the impact of clergy families and on clergy who are single.

UNREALISTIC EXPECTATIONS

When we work with congregations, whether for team building, vision discernment, or conflict, we often recognize the unrealistic expectations congregations have of their ministers and often that clergy have of themselves. I (Mary Kay) was accompanying a rural, two-point parish as they accepted a new young, single pastor into their parish. One of the congregations, though they contracted with him for only 40 percent of his time, expected that he attend every football game, graduation, community event, and the list went on. And they gave him, literally, a list. They attempted to write it into the contract. As I reflected with the pastor on the fact that the expectations were unrealistic, his response was, "Well, I want to do it because I really love these people." He would have worked himself to death if others hadn't been looking out for him. (The other congregation had much more realistic expectations.)

The weight of expectations becomes more difficult when they aren't actually written down—when a clergyperson tries in vain to meet an unrealistic and unspoken or unwritten vision for who they are supposed to be and what they are supposed to do. With unrealistic expectations, clergy can quickly begin to feel unworthy, causing them to retreat or try harder, only to fail and feel worse. On top of the long, grueling hours, the feelings of incompetence can cause clergy to feel quite lonely. One study revealed that occupational stress is reported when "work objectives are unclear, when they have conflicting demands placed on them, when they have too little or too much to do, when they have little input in decisions that affect them, and when they are responsible for other workers' development."[1] At LeaderWise, we see these stress factors at work time and time again.

When we (LeaderWise) see these unrealistic expectations at play, we immediately suggest a facilitated discussion between the clergy and congregation leaders around mutual expectations. In these holy conversations, congregations get to reflect on their true expectations for their clergy (as well as what's realistic) and clergy get to think about their true expectations for their congregation partners (as well as what's realistic). These conversations can be beautiful examples of compassion-filled dialogue that result in deeper understanding and relationships. Then we create a covenant that all parties sign. It provides a foundation for future conversations when conflict arises out of a mismatch in expectations. Simply having the mutual expectations conversation can begin to help clergy feel less shameful about their workload and set realistic boundaries and goals, allowing clergy to feel more competent. In our experience, when clergy feel competent, they are less likely to isolate themselves.

GOING WHERE THE CALLS ARE

If you are a Christian clergyperson, you likely trust the Holy Spirit is guiding your ministry. Many of us believe that the call to our vocation is more than just our passion for it, and so we listen, beyond our own wants and needs. We listen to trusted voices in the relationships that matter to us, we listen to the voices within congregations and judicatories that are seeking new pastors, and we listen for the leading of the Spirit. All this listening can lead us to take calls or appointments where we might not go if we were in a secular role. That is, we set aside our personal wants and needs because we feel that's what the Holy Spirit is calling us to do.

The result of taking calls where we might not otherwise have if we were in a different profession means we may move more often than people in secular roles, and we may end up in cultures quite different from those to which we are accustomed. A minister who has primarily lived in a city or suburb all their life can end up in a rural community, and vice versa. That can come with a steep cultural learning curve, along with extreme feelings of exclusion and isolation. Clergy who experience a more transient ministry express that they barely have time to establish deep relationships before they find themselves moving on to their next call.

It may seem like there isn't a whole lot one can do about this issue short of move to a place that's more comfortable. But you'll see in our next chapter on cognitive strategies that how we think about our experiences in general, and loneliness in particular, can help us feel quite differently.

THE NEED TO MAINTAIN BOUNDARIES

Tony and Louise came to LeaderWise for a two-day intensive program to discuss the recent dissolution of his call. They appeared a bit shell-shocked as they sat next to each other on the couch in my (Mark's) office, because just nine months earlier, their life in a remote Montana town seemed to be going well. They were heavily involved in the life of their town and counted many of the parishioners in Tony's three small congregations as friends. As Louise teared up, she declared, "I'm done! I'm not going through this heartbreak again. I thought these people were our friends." She acknowledged a deep sense of betrayal.

The change in relationships had come quickly, at least from Tony and Louise's perspective. One evening, the joint personnel committee, made up of members from the three congregations, proposed terminating Tony's call, and the proposal was later ratified by a churchwide vote among members from all three congregations. To be fair, only one of the three churches was really disgruntled, but it was by far the largest and carried the most weight. Tony was less certain than Louise about leaving ministry but felt equally hurt. Despite the emotional pain and

anger over the perceived injustice of how things were handled,
he wanted to at least consider the possibility of another call,
though he wasn't sure how one could serve a rural community
and not immerse oneself in the life of the community, includ-
ing developing friendships.

The idea of holding "healthy boundaries" is drilled into us from the time we begin our ministerial training until the end of our career (and even into retirement). Most denominations require that clergy take boundaries training courses every few years in order to remind themselves of the rules, regulations, and guidelines, as well as provide an opportunity to take a time out and examine their own boundary-related behaviors and decision-making ethics. While these trainings are good and helpful and we recommend them whole-heartedly, they also reinforce the separate nature of clergy's lives—that they are separate from their congregation and separate from the community at large.

One of the big boundary issues clergy face is how to be in relationship with people in their congregations and communities. Most clergy agree that having close friendships with people in congregations is not a good idea, but even clergy can disagree with one another about what is appropriate. For instance, how does a minister develop friendships in the community when the community is small or the clergyperson feels like they don't have time to devote to developing friendships? In these cases, the easiest path may be to share some level of friendship with members of their own congregation—though this likely comes with risks, as Tony and Louise discovered. Still, other clergy may discourage the loosening of the boundary between clergy and parishioners under any circumstance, and judicatory staff in particular may frown upon this, since they often have to deal with the aftermath of boundary crossings and violations. For clergy who already feel like they do not fit in, the debate itself can instill additional feelings of self-doubt and alienation, especially if they don't see many other options for making friends.

The complexity of boundaries is further heightened when a minister has a spouse or children, because each person in the clergy family may act independently in their individual relationships. At the same time, the family as a whole may need to navigate some complex boundary issues together (e.g., keeping quiet if they're considering a move, timing the announcement if they've accepted another appointment or call, dealing with conflict within their own family), and a spouse and children may be much less concerned about maintaining the sharp distinction between congregational relationships and friendships than the clergy parent. We discuss clergy families further later in the chapter.

When we work with ministers at LeaderWise, we emphasize the need to accept the set-apart nature of the role and to use cognitive strategies to do so (more on this in the next chapter). It is also very helpful for clergy quite specifically to think through where their boundaries are and to communicate those explicitly within their myriad relationships. One pastor told us the story of having coffee with a member of the local community (not a congregation member) who was becoming a friend. The community member began to ask for some advice. As they started into that conversation, the pastor wisely asked for a pause to discuss the boundaries of the conversation and the roles they each were playing. They agreed that in their coffee conversations, which had become dear to each of them, they were friends first. That helped them understand the boundaries of the conversation, and they both felt good about their decision and the way they'd reached it.

INABILITY TO BE AUTHENTIC

Sharon, a member of a focus group on loneliness, shared that when she was diagnosed with lymphoma, her doctor asked her if she'd consider attending a support group. Given the peculiarities of clergy life, Sharon felt it would be hard for nonclergy to understand her unique questions and struggles, such as how much to share with her congregation, who to ask to accompany her to doctor appointments, how to negotiate time off with her personnel committee, and the like. Because of this, Sharon asked her doctor if they knew of any clergy support groups rather than signing up for a general one. The doctor, intrigued by the specialized request, went to bat for her and searched across the country for an appropriate support group. The oncologist didn't find a single one anywhere in the country. Consequently, the pastor chose to go it alone rather than seek support from a general support group that

*she felt wouldn't understand this dominant part of her identity
and life.*

Because clergy often hold such strict boundaries in and
around their congregations, even if partnered they can feel
as though they don't have many, or any, intimate relationships in which they can truly be authentic and vulnerable.
This observation is borne out by our research too. Although
clergy score similarly to the general population for being
lonely, as we noted previously, the distinguishing factor
for them is their social isolation. Their role sets them apart,
and they feel significantly more alone, isolated, and separated
from others.

At the same time, we know that social support is perhaps the key ingredient for people's well-being. In addition
to the results of contemporary research on loneliness and
social belonging, which we discussed in chapter 2, the Grant
Study of Harvard University, a longitudinal study that has
tracked people across their lifetime, provides another window
into the importance of social support. The researchers followed the same group of 268 Harvard sophomores from the
1930s to the present and, as part of their protocol, assessed
their emotional and physical health at least every two years.
The study's primary conclusion was this: social support, by
far, is the component that best predicts both physical health
and emotional well-being across the life span. As George
Vaillant, a lead researcher in the study, famously stated when

asked about the secret to well-being based on their research, "The short answer is L-O-V-E."[2]

Where can ministers turn for emotional and social support? While it may be easy for clergy to live day to day ignoring their own needs and commonly overextending themselves for the sake of their ministry, over the long term they will likely pay a price for doing so. In the near term too, when a major life event happens to them or their loved ones, clergy can feel the acute pang of isolation as they are reminded that they have nowhere to turn—that they are set apart. In Emily's story at the beginning of this chapter, she even tried to turn to her judicatory staff and felt only shame when she did so. And Sharon's story describes how few understand the unique role of ministry and consequently how isolating that can feel in a clergyperson's time of need.

Emily's story, at the beginning of this chapter, is one we've heard over and over again. Clergy accompany their parishioners during the big events of the parishioners' lives. It is part of a clergyperson's call to ministry. As a matter of fact, most clergy will say that the tender moments in which clergy are invited into parishioners' lives are some of the best days to be in ministry and among the primary reasons they felt called to this profession. Being let in deeply to a parishioner's life during the hard times, and the joyous times, is an honor, and they wouldn't have it any other way.

Many clergy we talked with in our focus groups indicated that therapists, coaches, and spiritual directors are lifelines for them. These are great support systems, and we highly recommend them. And still, we all need intimate relationships, such as best friends, who we can count on to have our backs when we're in difficult situations and to hold us up when we're emotionally unable to do so ourselves.

THEOLOGICAL AND IDEOLOGICAL DIFFERENCES

In our conversations with clergy, we often hear stories about how they feel theologically, politically, and socially different from the people in their congregations. Clergy often have a different view from their parishioners of what it means to live out the gospel, and that difference can cause ministers to feel as though they can't show up authentically. For instance, clergy may view it as their responsibility to critique the social and political issues of the day from a theological perspective, while some parishioners may bristle at the slightest perception of the minister "preaching politics from the pulpit." Even the most carefully worded sermon on a heated issue can elicit negative reactions from congregation members who may have made assumptions about the minister's political or social views. Consequently, some ministers learn to play it safe by avoiding charged issues. They likely pay a price for such caution, though. If we can't show up authentically and say what we believe based on our theological studies, reflections, and convictions, we hide ourselves from others, which will undoubtedly generate feelings of loneliness. Further, when clergy hold back on their views, they can feel like they aren't being true to their theology, leaving them feeling as if they aren't fully living out their calling. This is another reason clergy benefit from safe places to be completely authentic and vulnerable. They need to wrestle with their theological, political, and social questions with others who understand them, and clergy peer groups and close clergy colleagues with whom we feel at ease provide such opportunities.

LaVonne, a pastor in one of our clergy loneliness support groups, shared with the other members about how she had been "doing her work" around racism after the murder of George Floyd. The isolation of the pandemic had given her emotional space from her parishioners to delve deeply into the history of racism in the United States, and she had arrived at a new understanding of the deeply entrenched nature of systematic racism. LaVonne felt like she was in a different place now from her congregation. She was worried about the implications of that for her ministry as the congregation began to gather in person again postpandemic. She didn't feel as though her congregation was ready to hear her views, and she worried they would realize her views about race had shifted, even if she didn't share too deeply. She also felt called to lead the congregation in this work because of her theological belief in loving all neighbors. LaVonne felt conflicted about the whole situation, and it contributed to her feelings of isolation and loneliness.

Occasionally, we'll meet with clergy who may feel in step with their congregation (theologically, politically, or socially) but feel out of step with their denominations. The larger culture wars of our society are often mirrored in debates on the floors of synods, conferences, assemblies, and other forums. When a vote is taken by a denomination on a controversial social issue, such as whether to allow same-sex marriages, clergy in the minority position can feel alienated from their colleagues, which can further fuel isolation and loneliness. If these clergy feel too marginalized, they may leave their denomination or ministry altogether. Without taking intentional steps to resolve them, feelings of resentment and bitterness can linger for years. We have found too that clergy who reach out to a spiritual director, coach, or counselor to talk through these experiences can benefit from the emotional support and a confidential place to reflect and can discover greater peace of mind.

THE CLERGY SPOUSE AND FAMILY

So far, we have been sharing some reasons clergy feel lonely and isolated. The research bears out that clergy families also experience loneliness and isolation because they too are set apart. Just as congregations have high expectations for clergy, they often have high expectations for spouses and families too. There was a time in the church when the wife (because at that time, the pastor was certainly a man) was an ever-present part of the ministry. This one-time cultural norm is still an expectation in many places. Additionally, children were and are supposed to be perfectly well behaved. These unrealistic expectations can place undue stress on all members of the clergy family.

One helpful study by E. Wayne Hill and colleagues revealed six primary issues that contribute to stress in clergy families: time, mobility, congregational fit, isolation, space, and intrusions.[3] While one of these, isolation, is directly related to loneliness, most of the others can also indirectly contribute to feelings of loneliness among clergy and their families.

Time

Clergy are always on call. This can interrupt valuable family time. Additionally, in our experience, because of clergy's strong sense of call, they have a hard time saying no to the demands of ministry. Given the high demand on their time, clergy have little time for a social life or hobbies, and their families express that their clergy loved one isn't around enough.

Mobility

We discussed this issue earlier in this chapter, focusing on the clergy's experience. Their families, of course, are also impacted by frequent moves. In the Hill study, the aspects of mobility that most affected families on the move were "children needing to orient to new neighborhoods, friends, and schools; moving costs; and the moving process itself. One clergy member stated that the most stressful thing about frequent moves was 'feeling as if I have no control over my destiny.'"[4] For clergy *and* their families, the need to repeatedly find and develop new friendships, if they even can, can feel overwhelming.

Congregational Fit

Trinity and First, a two-point parish, was in the process of calling a new pastor and was excited about having someone who could lead them into whatever the future would hold for this parish. The leaders talked of being ready to embrace change; they were ready to try new things. Pastor Juan, being an innovator at heart, seemed like a good fit for the congregation. But when he, after being in the parish for only three months, changed up the liturgy one Sunday, conflict ensued. When pressed, Juan said he thought changing worship slightly was a good warm-up to experimenting with the change they purported to want. When discussing the issues with the congregation, it was apparent they weren't ready at all for change of any kind. He was gone within a year and felt like a failure in the process.

No matter how hard all parties try to ensure a solid and strong fit between clergy and a congregation, at best it's an imperfect union and at worst an irreconcilable conflict waiting to tear the congregation apart. A mismatch in readiness for change isn't the only issue that contributes to a lack of congregational fit. In the study by Hill et al., other issues cited were "conflicts with and between staff members, and tensions between the clergy and the laity regarding differing theological beliefs, ideas, and philosophies." Betrayal of trust was also experienced, especially by the clergy spouse, and being compared to previously beloved pastors was also described by clergy in their focus groups.[5]

When a congregational relationship doesn't work out, it can feel nearly as heartbreaking as when a personal relationship ends. In these times, pastors can experience acute loneliness and subsequently isolate themselves from their support systems out of a sense of failure or shame. For some, it can be just too much to overcome, leading them to question whether they can continue in ministry at all.

A poor fit between the clergyperson and congregation can overflow to the family. In the Hill study, clergy spouses talked about the stress they experienced when their clergy spouse was struggling in the congregation because of fit. They described having to endure betrayals of trust, members turning on the family, and having to listen to criticism of their spouse.[6]

Isolation

In addition to clergy feeling lonely and isolated, spouses also report feeling isolated because they are automatically considered to be different from other people. Spouses also indicate that having to move far from family contributes to their own feelings of isolation. Further, in our experience, clergy will often not share deeply with their spouses about what is going on in their ministry. This is a healthy boundary, sparing the spouse all the details and also preventing triangulation, since the spouse also knows the congregation. However, this lack of opportunity to support their spouses can lead clergy spouses to feel left out too.

Space and Intrusions

While personal space and intrusions aren't directly related to loneliness and isolation, they do play a part. Since we wholeheartedly believe in solitude and Sabbath as remedies to the experience of loneliness (see part 3 of this book), having space to be alone with God is important. Clergy who live in parsonages or are well known in their communities can have difficulty finding spaces that allow them to be alone without intrusion. Many clergy who live in parsonages experience the severe boundary crossing of members entering the home uninvited. One clergyperson told a story that she was napping on the couch one Sunday afternoon (a healthy thing for clergy to do!), and she woke to the sound of keys jangling in the lock of her front door. In walked a family who wanted to show the parsonage to their relatives. Unfortunately, this story isn't a unique one. Further, if the minister is well known in their community, even things like going to the gym for a workout become hard to do without having to "be on" as a minister. Going back to the Hill study, they repeatedly emphasized the importance of clarity and communication about boundaries. When clergy families together set their boundaries and communicate them, they can enjoy greater well-being.

THE SINGLE LIFE

Finally, we would be remiss if we didn't pay attention to clergy who have chosen to lead an unpartnered life. Often, when a clergyperson goes to seminary right after completing their bachelor's degree, they either meet their future partner in seminary or find themselves in their first call as a single person. An older seminarian likewise may struggle with isolation and loneliness if they relocate without a partner, often with family and friends far afield. Some clergy also choose to remain single. While partnered clergy might feel lonely because they are trying to spare their partners all the details, single clergy often feel even more so, not having anyone on whom they can depend day in and day out.

We have heard story after story about single clergy who, wanting to find a life partner, will not reveal their profession for fear that the (potential) date will be a nonstarter. In our experience, this is particularly true for women clergy. Most first dates happen through online dating apps these days, and people make assumptions about who a clergyperson is simply because of their title. Add to this the fact that many clergy find themselves in small towns where it's difficult to meet potential dating partners, and finding a mate can feel like an impossibility. Finally, many clergy experience people in their congregations trying to play matchmaker, leaving the clergyperson trying gently time and time again to help the well-intentioned and misguided congregant understand the inappropriateness of that gesture. It's especially important for single clergy to have those spaces where they can be authentic and fill their soul with the compassion and love of others who understand them. This is a statement we've made several times, and it goes to show how important those spaces are. The metaphor of what goes on during a theater production can be helpful here.

FRONT STAGE, BACKSTAGE, OFFSTAGE

For over a decade, Matt Bloom and colleagues, as part of the Flourishing in Ministry project at Notre Dame University, have studied several thousand clergy from various denominations to determine what contributes to well-being among them. As a helpful metaphor, they have compared a life in ministry to being an actor in the theater and examined the experiences of being on the front stage, in the backstage, and offstage.[7]

The front stage is the place where we are on display and fully functioning as a clergyperson. All eyes are on us in these very public spaces—worship, meetings, pastoral care, mission work, being out in the community, and so forth. Additionally, the world and those closest to us have expectations for how we show up within our identity as clergy. These include the expectations we've already discussed about what clergy *should do*. People also have expectations about how a clergyperson *should be*. For clergy to feel like they can show up authentically when on the front stage can be difficult. The more a clergyperson can show up authentically in this space, however, the more resilient they will be.

In theater, the backstage is the support space that makes everything on the front stage run seamlessly and effortlessly. In ministry, backstage is the place where we gather with colleagues we trust deeply to wrestle with all the ups and downs of ministry and to give and receive careful, compassionate, and honest feedback. Our backstage is a place where we can show up authentically, be vulnerable, and get the support we need. While in the backstage, clergy can recharge their batteries and get a fresh perspective on ministry. Common examples of backstage experiences include mentoring relationships, other one-on-one supportive relationships, sermon preparation and worship planning with other clergy in our communities, and clergy peer groups within our denominations. When starting out in ministry, backstage experiences are essential for us to develop a ministerial and denominational identity, and if these experiences are missing, we can experience professional isolation and discouragement and sometimes leave ministry prematurely. Bloom identifies the characteristics of a good backstage:

- It offers a space to reflect on what is happening on the front stage, so clergy can improve their performance on the front stage.
- It provides support and care for the clergy in the group.

- It provides an environment in which the clergy can develop well. It serves as a space of accountability and honest feedback.[8]

Offstage is the space where we as clergy can completely take off our professional identity and be vulnerable with trusted friends and family. Not only are we not performing the role in any way; the goal is to not think about the role at all. While offstage, we engage in hobbies and spend time in the company of deeply loved ones.

In our work, we see too many clergy who don't have enough time offstage, as evidenced by feelings of exhaustion and burnout. If this is your situation, Chris Adams, a researcher with the Flourishing in Ministry research program, recommends a straightforward intervention that you can practice almost immediately. At the end of your work day today, take fifteen minutes to do something you love for the sheer pleasure of it, regardless of its relevance for your ministry context. Call a friend, read a funny piece, laugh at a comedy skit, walk outside to unwind, or just breathe in and out. Get offstage.[9]

Some of this discussion may feel overwhelming. After all, if you are a minister trying to do the right thing by holding strict relational boundaries, what on earth can you do about the natural consequence of feeling isolated and lonely? The good news is, there *are* things each of us can do to reduce the feelings of loneliness and isolation. Part 2 of the book concentrates on remedies with which each of us can experiment. We've given you a taste of them throughout this chapter, and in the next, we will dive deeper. We fully believe that with a bit of intentionality, you will be on your way to feeling more socially connected in no time.

FOR REFLECTION AND DISCUSSION

1. To what parts of this discussion of the clergy life do you most relate? Why?
2. Who is on your backstage, and how do you have that trusted space structured?
3. What remedies have you tried for some of the causes of loneliness discussed in this chapter?

PART II

Paths to Belonging

There are many remedies to loneliness and social isolation, including cognitive strategies (changing the ways we think), spiritual practices, intentionally building relationships, and the like. The research will tell you that any one of them will put you on the path to belonging, so you don't have to adopt three or five or all these approaches (and add to your already over loaded to-do list). So as you read and wonder about your own life, be gentle with yourself. Be realistic about what you can add to your life, and choose those ideas that seem most doable.

A shared theme among all these strategies is that they emphasize life-giving practices that foster positive emotions, which help us move through loneliness and isolation toward a sense of wholeness and belonging. Martin Seligman, one of the foremost researchers of clinical depression in the twentieth century, had a pivotal experience late in his career that led him to become one of the founders of a movement to research the cultivation of positive emotions, which has become known as the positive psychology movement. While weeding his garden one day, he became irritated with Nikki, his six-year-old daughter. He explains,

> I am goal oriented and time urgent, and when I'm weeding in the garden, I'm actually trying to get the weeding done. Nikki, however, was throwing weeds into the air, singing, and dancing around. I yelled at her. She walked away, then came back and said,
>
> "Daddy, I want to talk to you."
>
> "Yes, Nikki?"
>
> "Daddy, do you remember before my fifth birthday? From the time I was three to the time I was five, I was a whiner. I whined every day. When I turned five, I decided not to whine anymore. That was the hardest thing I've ever done. And if I can stop whining, you can stop being such a grouch."[1]

Seligman comments, "This for me was an epiphany, nothing else." He elaborates that it led him to shift his focus in his research, as well as in his life, from centering on negative emotions to positive emotions. His subsequent research, along with that of numerous colleagues, demonstrated that Nikki was correct—we can actively work to transform our less desirable emotional states to more desirable ones.

Barbara Fredrickson, a researcher who has studied the origins and purpose of positive emotions, further explains that positive emotional states tend to build upon one another. Drawing upon her *broaden-and-build theory* of positive emotions, Fredrickson's research demonstrates that one positive emotional state often serves as the catalyst for additional positive emotional states, which can result in an upward spiral of life-enhancing emotions. This is good news, considering the downward spiral effect loneliness can have on a person. Specifically, Fredrickson's research indicates that positive emotions "(i) broaden people's attention and thinking; (ii) undo lingering negative emotional arousal; (iii) fuel psychological resilience; (iv) build consequential personal resources; (v) trigger upward spirals towards greater well-being in the future; and (vi) seed human flourishing."[2] Based on her findings, Fredrickson speaks directly to us: "People should cultivate positive emotions in their own lives and in the lives of those around them, not just because doing so makes them feel good in the moment, but also because doing so transforms people for the better and sets them on paths toward flourishing and healthy longevity."[3]

Any action you take to address loneliness and isolation can generate positive emotional states, and the process toward greater well-being will be set in motion. So if you have the energy for a few changes in your life, by all means, go for it! And as always when embarking on incorporating new habits into your life, we also encourage you to reflect on what you can give up to make space for the new ways of being. What no longer serves you well?

Our invitation to you is to pick something that feels doable and stick with it. Any life-giving practice to overcome loneliness is worthwhile, as it will likely cultivate positive emotions and lead to greater well-being. This may then contribute to additional energy and motivation and lead you to take up another remedy to try.

Learning to Think Differently

"We often wait for kindness . . . but being kind to yourself can start now," said the mole.

—Wisdom from Charlie Mackesy,
The Boy, the Mole, the Fox, and the Horse

Matthew, a forty-one-year-old single man serving a church in a small midwestern town, felt isolated and lonely. Having grown up, gone to college, and attended seminary in California, he now found himself on the great plains, half a continent away from his support system of family and friends. In fact, he was two hours away from the next town of any size and the opportunity to meet people outside of his congregation who could become friends. His mood and job performance had both slipped in recent months as he dealt with a pervasive sense of isolation. He was also full of self-recrimination, bemoaning,

"How could I be so stupid! I gave up California—everything I love—to come to a land with no trees, no friends . . . and no fun." Because he was serving his first church as a pastor, he was also fearful that he would sacrifice future opportunities if he left after only a couple of years. Besides, he thought, even in the future, what church in California would ever take him again after serving in the Midwest, where the culture and values are vastly different? He felt as if he was destined to languish the rest of his career.

FOR REFLECTION

- To what part of Matthew's story do you relate?
- What advice would you give Matthew about his predicament?

At LeaderWise, we've taken to talking about loneliness—a lot. Our goal is for it to be top of mind so we can help people identify, describe, and discuss it. At our workshops on clergy health and well-being, we are matter-of-fact about all aspects of ministry, including loneliness. In one exercise, we have people line up, making a human continuum. We give them a number of statements, and they move, on the continuum, to a location that corresponds to their reaction to how true the statement is for them. For example, we might state "I feel satisfied in ministry," "I feel hopeful in ministry," or "Ministry excites me," with "Very true" on one end of the room, "Sometimes" in the middle, and "Not at all true" on the other end.

After building trust in the group, we introduce statements that are riskier and test participants' emotional vulnerability, such as "Sometimes I question my call to ministry" and "I feel lonely in ministry."

When we first began asking about loneliness, we weren't sure what to expect. We knew the statistics from national studies on the general population, as well as our own data, and researchers have legitimately described loneliness in the general population of the United States as "an epidemic." We wondered, though, whether participants would share their experiences of loneliness with their peers or would keep mum out of a sense of vulnerability and, possibly, shame. We discovered that people in our workshops were honest, and poignantly so. At one workshop, as a sizable cluster gathered around "Very true" for "I feel lonely in ministry," participants began to open up about their experiences. One clergyperson talked about the struggles of living in a small town as a young single adult; another shared the loneliness of being a middle-aged woman in ministry who was recently divorced; and a third pastor, who served a large church in a medium-sized town and by all accounts was a popular and effective pastor, confessed, "I'm really, really lonely."

In this exercise, as well as in our one-on-one conversations, we've noticed that people struggle for words to express their experiences of loneliness. They feel it profoundly, knowing it's there, but they can't quite articulate it. Part of the issue is that loneliness is a misunderstood emotion. From an early age, many of us are taught by parents, family members, and teachers to identify feelings of happiness and sadness, and perhaps other emotions, through pointing at or drawing faces on a sheet of paper. But how many of us are taught to identify, understand, or name loneliness with any frequency? We lack practice in recognizing the various shades of loneliness and talking out loud about it. Further, loneliness looks different for each person. So if we were to tell a friend that we feel lonely, they might say, "But you have so many friends and you're always so busy!" Reactions like this can lead us to question whether our feelings are justified, and we may begin to keep our thoughts and feelings to ourselves.

Finally, loneliness has a stigma attached to it too. Studies indicate that the primary fuel of loneliness, once it appears, is our own sense of shame. We tend to believe there's something wrong with us if we're lonely, and we ignore the fact that almost half the population also reports feeling sometimes or always "left out," "alone," or "like no one knows them well."[1] According to recent research, we blame ourselves for our loneliness—as if there's something inherently wrong with us—and we tend to doubt that our social situation will ever improve. We view loneliness as a stable, immutable, and unending condition for ourselves, extending out as far as we can see.[2] The result? Our loneliness only intensifies and exacerbates our negative thinking, which contributes to further feelings of loneliness.

The good news is, we can break this downward spiral of loneliness and negative thinking. In fact, research shows that changing the way we talk and think about our loneliness is the most effective way to begin to shift from loneliness to well-being.[3] In psychology, we talk about cognitive strategies. A cognitive strategy is an intentional process for shifting one's thinking in order to change one's perception. In the rest of this chapter, we describe some cognitive strategies that we've found most helpful in our work with people who are lonely.

MINDFULNESS

Mindfulness has garnered a lot of attention in recent years as a way to manage a variety of life concerns, including stress, anxiety, depression, chronic pain, and other issues. We find it's especially helpful for addressing loneliness. Because we lack practice in naming and talking about our experience of loneliness, we're at a bit of a loss on how to recognize and work with it. The feeling of loneliness is unpleasant, and our first inclination might very well be to shut it down and step back from our experience of it. Ironically, this avoidance is the very thing that can most intensify it. We now feel separated from not only others but ourselves too.

Mindfulness is a practice that enables us to live into our experience of loneliness in the present moment. In mindfulness, we always emphasize that whatever thoughts we are having in the moment are OK; we aren't to judge them or rid ourselves of them. Ultimately, this approach enables us to meet, accept, and find peace in the midst of our loneliness. We consciously remember, and remind ourselves, that feelings are just feelings and that they come and go quickly if we simply observe them without judgment. In fact, psychologists have found that our emotions, which are based on fleeting physiological states, typically last "a matter of seconds or at most minutes."[4] While loneliness can be an ongoing experience, the acute pain of loneliness—that sudden pang you feel in being left out—passes rather quickly if you call your attention to it and observe the intensity of the ebb and flow.

One mindfulness technique is to view your emotions as clouds passing in the sky. The brilliance of the sky and warmth of the sun are always present, though they can be temporarily blocked by storm clouds; they will reappear once the winds shift and the clouds pass through. If you step back, breathe deeply, and observe loneliness—without judging yourself or the experience—you'll see that in the moment, it's only a passing emotion.

With practice, mindfulness can become an approach to life too. With mindfulness, we experience the world differently, simply observing the wide range of emotions we experience as they come and go. After all, our lives are made up of a series of moments, and we can practice one moment as passing and another moment as emerging, which offers new possibilities for engaging the world in fresh ways over the long term.

As a result, when we begin to practice mindfulness, it often leads to behavioral change. We begin to recognize that our past or current unhappiness does not need to be our destiny. When loneliness appears, in the next moment we can begin anew to address it through reaching out to friends, family, or colleagues; making different life choices; or engaging in a life-giving activity.

RAIN

Tara Brach, a psychologist and mindfulness teacher, has created a helpful acronym, RAIN, which offers a structured approach to mindfulness.[5] RAIN stands for Recognize, Allow, Investigate, Nurture, and she lays out the framework this way:

> Recognize what is happening.
>
> Allow the experience to be there, just as it is.
>
> Investigate with interest and care.
>
> Nurture with self-compassion.

In an individual session, Matthew, whom you met at the beginning of this chapter, and I (Mark) practiced RAIN. As Matthew walked through the acronym, the following thoughts and feelings emerged.

Recognize

In our sessions together, Matthew came to view the full scope of his social isolation and loneliness—the feelings, thoughts, and behaviors that accompany it. He shared, "I'm tired—and, of course, lonely. I also feel discouraged and hopeless about the situation ever improving."

To add more nuance and better understand the contours of loneliness, we'll often ask where a person experiences it in their body. Matthew observed, "I feel it like a pressure behind my eyes and a lump in my throat. I want to cry, but it almost feels too big to let it happen." By pausing and taking stock, he also found himself wanting to change the subject, which he could recognize as a common pattern of trying to distract himself whenever feelings of loneliness and isolation intensified.

Allow

We also ask people to stay present with an emotion, even if it is unpleasant. Although it was uncomfortable, Matthew stayed attuned to his feeling of loneliness when it became acute, and he practiced accepting it. He experimented with saying to himself, "Yes, loneliness, it makes sense you're here. I'm far from family and friends. You are part of my life right now." By allowing his loneliness to remain fully present each time it visited, he came to see there was no need to fear it, that it took up the right amount of space and he wasn't consumed or overwhelmed by it.

Investigate

Our emotions are signals to us to take a moment, step back, and pay attention, because they emerge for a reason. By creating space for his loneliness, Matthew could now approach it with curiosity. He inquired, "Loneliness, what are you trying to tell me? You visit often, and I really want to know what you'd like me to learn from you. What wise advice do you have for me?" In this case, Matthew discovered that loneliness was telling him to make some life changes to reconnect with family and friends and to seriously consider a plan to return to California.

Nurture Self-Compassion

Sitting with loneliness, as with any emotional or physical pain, can be difficult and challenging. As we do the RAIN practice, the last step, to nurture self-compassion, is crucial. Despite being a bit self-conscious, Matthew placed his hand on his heart and whispered to himself, "It's OK, Matthew, we all feel lonely at times." He added, "I'm listening to you and love you. We all want what's best for you. If returning to California will help, then do it. I know God wants what is best for you too. God loves you deeply, Matthew."

AFTER THE RAIN

Tara Brach adds one more step to this process that she calls "After the RAIN." After moving through the RAIN exercise for loneliness (or any difficult emotion), take a moment to rest in your awareness. What are you experiencing (thinking, feeling, or doing) right now? Typically, by creating space for your emotions and practicing greater self-acceptance, you'll notice a calm in both your mind and body and a deep sense of well-being.

I (Mary Kay) spent a lot of pandemic time working from my husband's and my north woods cabin. Our cabin is remote, in the middle of a national forest, so my husband and I can go for days (or weeks) without seeing anyone else in person (thank you, video conferencing!). One day, I was feeling particularly off, though I wasn't aware that loneliness was the emotion I was having. I *recognized* it after I had been feeling a bit teary and crabby. I took some time and *allowed* the feelings to just be with me, which helped me figure out that it was loneliness that I was feeling. Normally, I would try to push it away, pretend it wasn't real, and most likely just hunker down and get back to work. After all, I shouldn't experience loneliness when I have a loving husband with me all the time! But this time I let it stay with me. As I *investigated* my emotion, questioning why I could feel so down when I love this place so much and look forward to my time here, I remembered reading a study once that talked about how critical female relationships are to women. Just as loneliness is detrimental to our health, for women the lack of female relationships is equally detrimental. Remembering this, I could *nurture* myself with compassion. And I decided to take the step to share with my husband that I was feeling down because I was missing girlfriend time. After acknowledging this, we took a walk, and I realized thirty minutes later that I was feeling much better. By going through the process and identifying what was really going on, I could choose a healthy next step: I reached out to some friends to set up some dates to happen when I returned from the cabin. Having those on my calendar gave me something to look forward to, and I felt better.

MENTAL REFRAMING

Mental reframing is a time-honored strategy used by psychologists to help us check out the accuracy of our thoughts and perceptions and to "reframe" (reinterpret) them in a way that's more balanced and life affirming. Like mindfulness and the RAIN approach, mental reframing is based on the premise that emotions are important, in that they invite us to pay attention, and yet we understand they are also ephemeral, as they are not the sum total of our experience. In other words, they do not define us, and in fact, our thoughts that give rise to painful emotions, such as loneliness, might even be inaccurate. For instance, have you ever felt the sting of being left out of a social occasion by a friend or loved one, brooded on the perceived slight over an extended period, only to find out later that there was a plausible explanation—at least from the other person's perspective?

As clergy, we experience being left out quite a bit. As much as we'd like to be included in certain social gatherings, others can perceive us as "different" or "set apart," to use theological language, and may choose not to invite us. They may believe we'd be uncomfortable or might not fit in. Anna, a thirty-seven-year-old married mother of two small children, served a small church in a medium-sized suburb. She loved living in her suburban neighborhood, where the mothers of young children would gather in the park to socialize while the kids played. Once a month, this group of women traveled to the city to eat out and have a drink for "girls' night out." Anna was caught off guard, and she felt her breath temporarily taken away, when another woman in the neighborhood shared that the group recently spent a weekend at a lakeside cabin. She heard about their moonlight boat excursion and their talking late into the night while sipping glasses of wine. Anna was struck by their brazenness in talking openly about the weekend in front of her. Her thoughts cascaded from "Did I miss the email invitation?" to "I would have loved this" to "I can't believe they didn't invite me" to "I thought they were my friends!" She recognized the familiar pain of feeling excluded, which she attributed to people's concern that she might be "too good" to enjoy a fun time.

In a clergy support group, Anna shared her experience. Heads nodded as others recognized a familiar dynamic. One told about feeling left out when they learned about their friends' monthly all-night poker sessions, which they heard about only through the grapevine. Another commiserated by talking about how her schedule prevented her from joining friends for dinner on the weekends, when they were off work but her ministry schedule ramped up, and about how the invitations stopped coming after a while. Making things worse, the group noted that a minister's day off often happens when their friends go back to work. Through this conversation, Anna came to recognize that her experience was quite common among ministers. In fact, our LeaderWise survey found that the most prominent form of loneliness is personal/individual isolation, in which a person feels cut off from others and excluded. The conversation and support of her clergy colleagues helped Anna reframe her experience from being about her, as if she were somehow deficient in social skills or flawed in her personality, to being "set apart," rightly or wrongly, due to her role. Anna was able to gain some "cognitive distance," or a broader perspective on her relationship with the women in the neighborhood, to not take her exclusion personally. They were merely misguided; Anna knew she could be a lot of fun!

Sometimes mental reframing can occur naturally through conversation with others, as our friends or colleagues help us place events in context and normalize our experiences. After conversations like this, things often don't seem as dire. Other times, having a framework for such reflection or conversation is helpful. Martin Seligman, who has studied how thinking affects our emotions, recommends the following four questions to help us check the accuracy of our perceptions and reframe our thoughts:

1. Is there evidence to support our interpretation of events?
2. Is there an alternative explanation besides our interpretation?

3. Is it really that bad even if our interpretation is correct?

4. Is it useful to think this way?[6]

Anna was fortunate to have a supportive colleague group to help her think through her experience, and Seligman's four questions can help us when we need to ponder things on our own. If she had come to LeaderWise, she might very well have heard about how to use these questions to check out the accuracy of her thoughts and gain a broader perspective. Using Anna's experience, and particularly a thought like "I guess they must not be my friends," we might have come up with something like the following.

Question: Is there evidence to support "I guess they must not be my friends"?

Anna's Response: While it's true that they didn't invite me on this one trip, they've consistently included me in other activities. We look after one another's kids, and we often chat on the phone and spontaneously get together. The preponderance of the evidence is that we act and care for one another like friends.

Question: Is there an alternative explanation besides "I guess they must not be friends"?

Anna's Response: Well, they might have thought that I'd be busy on the weekend given my job as a church pastor. In fact, they mentioned to me that it was a spur-of-the-moment decision, and I had told them about a big event at church that weekend, so they didn't bother to ask. It would have been better if they had asked, but I can understand their perspective.

Question: Is it really that bad if their friendship isn't as close as I had hoped?

Anna's Response: Well, yes, this would hurt a lot. At the same time, I have other close friendships that date back to college, so I do have another support system. I knew those friends before becoming a pastor and know that they'll be my community for life.

Question: Is it useful to think this way, "I guess they must not be friends"?

Anna's Response: It's not helpful at all! It just makes me feel mostly lonely—and also sad and angry. It's not worth dwelling on this thought. I'd much rather enjoy time with them rather than resent them, whether or not we're close friends. If nothing else, we're great neighbors for this period in our lives as we raise our children together.

KEEPING IN MIND ONE'S
LARGER CONNECTEDNESS

When we're lonely, we may turn inward. We set aside the very act that would help—namely, reaching out to others for support—because we don't want to risk rejection or feel left out again. Even making a phone call or inviting someone to an activity can stir unpleasant emotions because it reminds us of our sense of isolation. We feel vulnerable and tender. For those of us in ministry, it's often emotionally easier to compartmentalize our pain and lose ourselves in our role.

A final cognitive approach that can take the edge off the acute pain of loneliness and help us sidestep the trap of compartmentalization is simply to keep in mind our larger connections. Thich Nhat Hanh, a Buddhist monk, coined the word *inter-are*.[7] Everyone and everything is interrelated, and nothing exists independently from anything else. Without becoming overly metaphysical, "You are because I am, and I am because you are." Just as there can be no left without a right, no up without a down, there also can be no me without a you. We need each other just to exist!

While this might sound a bit abstract or metaphysical, it can have a practical application too. Reminding oneself that we're all interconnected can lessen the intensity of social isolation. As Thich Nhat Hanh points out, when we eat our cereal in the morning, it connects us to the sun and rain that nourished the grain, the farmer who harvested it, the factory workers who turned it into cereal, the food delivery people who shipped it, and the grocery workers who placed it on the shelves. And that's before we even pour the milk on it! In fact, we're really not alone at all as we sit down to consume our breakfast. To bring this to mind, we can pause and say a prayer of gratitude to remind us of our connection to all elements, people, and creatures that made this food possible.

After considering this idea of inter-are, Thea, a twenty-eight-year-old single woman who attended a retreat for newly ordained clergy, had an epiphany. In a small group conversation, she suddenly lit up and shared an insight: "It helps me think about a couple of really difficult people who are giving me a hard time in my congregation." She added, "As a former biology major, I just realized that we share 99.9 percent of the same DNA. We literally are the same person! If I hate them, I hate myself; if I love them, I love myself. It's helping me give them a bit more grace. Just like me, they want what's best for the church."

If you wish to go a step further, you can consider how much we inter-are with all creatures. For instance, scientists have found that we share 98 percent of our DNA with gorillas, chimpanzees, and pigs; 90 percent with our pet cats; and 84 percent with our dogs. And with that banana on our cereal, a solid 40 percent.[8]

Cognitive strategies are a great start for anyone experiencing a range of emotions around loneliness. As we embark on a path to belonging, we need to reflect on what it means to belong. The next chapter will explore this topic.

FOR REFLECTION AND DISCUSSION

1. This chapter shared a few stories of clergy who were experiencing loneliness and isolation. Which stories did you resonate with and why?

2. Thinking about a situation in your past or present, try employing one of the cognitive strategies in this chapter. What was the result?

3. Which cognitive strategy seems hardest for you? Why?

5

The Essentials of Belonging

The world feels high lonesome and heartbroken to me right now. We've sorted ourselves into factions based on our politics and ideology. We've turned away from one another and toward blame and rage. We're lonely and untethered. And scared. So damn scared.

—Brené Brown, *Braving the Wilderness*

Love each other as I have loved you.

—Jesus, John 15:12 NIV

In and through community lies the salvation of the world.

—M. Scott Peck, *The Different Drum*

Each member of the "loneliness and belonging group" popped up on the screen for our monthly seventy-five-minute Zoom call. These clergy had responded to our open invitation to any minister who wished to join, and we made it clear that we would limit the group to the first half dozen who responded. By now, after several months, the group had bonded.

At our check-in, Clarissa appeared stressed and tired, and she acknowledged, "I'm exhausted." She is a bivocational minister, serving a small congregation and running a farm. She also has three school-age children, ranging from third grade to high school. Clarissa began to tear up as she described her week. In addition to the demands of the church, it was birthing season for the goats on her farm. Dozens were being born in a matter of a couple of weeks. She remarked, "They just keep coming." It further broke her heart that she and her spouse couldn't keep up and some were dying. To complicate matters, her older children offered only a halfhearted effort to help with the goats, choosing to slip out of the house to be with friends whenever possible. She felt tired, frustrated, angry, and overwhelmed.

The group kicked in. Her colleagues, who had become friends in a matter of months, listened empathically and offered words of support. People expressed concern and encouraged her to take time to sleep and pace herself. The tears kept flowing. Then Mary spoke up, "Clarissa, where exactly in Nebraska do you live? I'm wondering if I can drive over and help." Mary lived in Chicago and had little familiarity with farm life. Summer, who had just completed training as a coach, expressed concern for Clarissa's well-being in trying to balance ministry, motherhood, and farming, and she offered to meet with Clarissa as a safe person with whom to discuss stress, boundaries, and self-care. Clarissa expressed heartfelt gratitude for all the support.

A year later, our group was reviewing their time together and what it had meant to them. Several identified the group as being instrumental in giving them a sense of belonging and a solid base to make positive changes in their life. Clarissa too, appearing rested and calm, referred to the group as a lifeline, giving her hope and a regular practice of self-care.

FOR REFLECTION

- What group do you have in which you could allow yourself to be as vulnerable as Clarissa was?
- If you don't have a group, how might you go about creating one?

From a theological perspective, we understand that God always intends for us to be in relationship. Those faith traditions that believe in a triune God understand this three-in-one God to be a living example of what this means. Salvation promises, finally, a never-again-separate communion with the Divine and with all creation. Where we fail to find belonging on this earth, we will finally experience the fullness of it in eternity.

What is belonging, anyway? The need to belong, or belongingness, is an inherent emotional need to feel like part of a group. More than just membership in a group, belonging is to give and receive attention. Abraham Maslow's hierarchy of needs places love and belonging squarely in the middle of the pyramid, after physiological needs (food, water, air, and so forth) and safety needs (personal security, secure employment, and the like). Psychologists Roy Baumeister and Mark Leary suggest that belongingness is so fundamental a need that severe consequences—such as mental distress, feelings of loneliness, and a lack of general well-being—arise when we lack a sense of belonging.[1]

Once again, we examine the assumption one could make that clergy have a built-in community in which their need to belong could be satisfied. Our research and experience state that it's just not true. Satisfying the need to belong requires more than merely being part of a group and even more than giving and receiving attention.

To build out a model for belonging, Michelle Lim, Kelly-Ann Allen, and colleagues have drawn on the widely accepted cognitive discrepancy theory of loneliness, which they summarize as a "subjective feeling of social isolation that arises when there is a difference between actual and desired relationships."[2] They define belonging broadly as being part of a place or experience. That is, belonging is a *subjective feeling* of being connected to a group of people, an experience, or a physical place. When we feel that we belong, we feel a level of comfort and satisfaction.

One could think about loneliness and belonging as the two poles on a continuum. If you feel you belong, you are probably not lonely. Therefore, it would make sense that these two human experiences are opposites. However, Lim and Allen propose a more complex relationship that looks like figure 5.1.[3] This more complex relationship provides a nuance that is often lacking when we think about loneliness. That is, what some might experience as loneliness, others might not, and we might experience loneliness in different ways depending on our desire for social connection. The model takes into account that we all have different preferences, based on our genetics and individual experiences, for social connectedness.

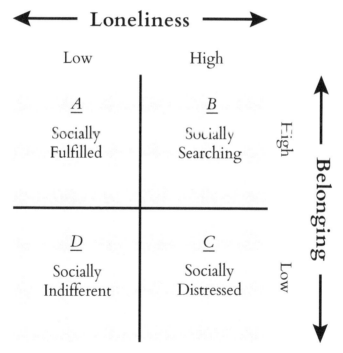

Figure 5.1. Lim and Allen's model of belonging and loneliness

If you have a low sense of loneliness (you rarely feel lonely) and a high sense of belonging (you have the spaces and relationships that fulfill you), Lim and Allen would place you in the category of socially fulfilled. In the opposing quadrant, if you feel pretty lonely most of the time and also don't feel like you belong anywhere, you would be socially distressed. We (Mark and Mary Kay) do not place a lot of judgments and labels on people's experiences; they are what they are. However, this model is helpful in the way it expresses the range of possibilities in the realm of loneliness and belonging.

There's still more nuance to this idea of belonging. Not only do we need to feel like we have groups, experiences, or places to which we belong, but we also need to feel like we truly *fit in*. We want to be accepted for who we are. When we have a sense of belonging, we understand we don't need to say or do what's expected by the group but can show up as our authentic selves. It's a rare setting in which anyone, let alone a clergyperson, can do this. (As a clergyperson, when was the last time you were in a setting in which you weren't checking the exact words you used, let alone the messages you were sending?) And when we spend months and years showing up in ways others expect, constantly checking ourselves, and then modifying our behavior, we sometimes lose our sense of self and who we truly are. When this happens, we become lonely and feel like we don't even belong to ourselves (let alone any other person or group). Our work is to first feel so comfortable in our own skin that we feel strong whether we are alone or in a group, even when that group has expectations of us that don't necessarily jive with our expectations of ourselves.

TRUE BELONGING

Brené Brown, in her book *Braving the Wilderness*, offers a definition of *true belonging*, which is a nuance of *belonging*: "True belonging is the spiritual practice of believing in and belonging to yourself so deeply that you can share your most authentic self with the world and find sacredness in both being a part of something and standing alone in the wilderness. True belonging doesn't require you to *change* who you are; it requires you to *be* who you are."[4]

This true belonging is not the same as rugged individualism, which is more about the myth of every person for themselves. True belonging begins with being in right relationship with ourselves—believing thoroughly in ourselves and what we stand for without compromising our authenticity, freedom, or power. If we can't achieve that, we'll never find true belonging anywhere else. Brown goes on to say that this deep sense of belonging can be a wilderness place (hence the title of her book). It is "an untamed, unpredictable place of solitude and searching. It is a place as dangerous as it is breathtaking, a place as sought after as it is feared."[5]

At this point, you might be thinking truly belonging is incredibly difficult to achieve in our divided society. Or you might be thinking about how difficult it is to show up authentically in your life experiences, and so you wonder, what's the point of even trying? Or you might be feeling a sense of dread or fear at just the thought of trying to show up authentically. It can quickly become a nonstarter.

Part of true belonging is understanding truly and deeply that you are a beloved child of God. It takes a lot of self-love to believe that and to live it from your core. Contemporary psychologists, such as Kristin Neff, often refer to this as the practice of self-compassion.[6] At this level of self-love, you treat yourself just like you'd treat your best friend. That means recognizing your brain's negative self-talk and reframing it, knowing and speaking your truth with love, and not compromising your integrity. Once we live that way, we become a model for others with the hope that they too will feel a deep sense of true belonging.

Dan, a counseling client, sat on the couch in my (Mark's) office and spoke in tones of self-judgment and self-blame, recalling the numerous mistakes he had made in the pastoral role. He felt a need to meet everyone's needs and please others, and he worked extra hard to measure his words and keep people happy. When someone was mad at him, it weighed heavily on him and sapped him of his joy for ministry. He would alternate between frustration with them and self-doubt as a leader.

In our time together, the topic of God's grace came up, and he talked about his desire to have everyone know that they are beloved children of God. I saw my opening: "What about you, Dan? It seems like you are so giving and concerned about the well-being of others, but you're quite harsh when you talk about yourself, especially if people are critical of you. Does God's grace include you too?"

Dan paused, teared up, and softly said, "Yes." We explored how Dan, although he might receive pushback and upset some people, is also a beloved child of God and how his voice matters as much as anyone's. He could express his theological views and be true to himself in the ministerial role. There is liberation in knowing that we can rest secure in God's grace, that we can be true to our convictions. God will stand by us through it all and will forgive us when we make mistakes.

Part of true belonging (and we need to learn this as a society in order to heal the divisions, cracks, and fissures with which we now live as a culture) is learning to be vulnerable—to enter into, or create, spaces in which courageous vulnerability can happen and then be received with compassion, curiosity, and acceptance. Brown goes so far as to say, "True belonging has no bunkers. We have to step out from behind the barricades of self-preservation and brave the wild."[7] Further, we must learn how to navigate conflict in healthy and open ways, seeing conflict as an opportunity for transformation rather than something to be feared and avoided. Conflict done poorly divides and isolates us. Healthy conflict has the potential to bring people together—to deepen relationships.

In Brown's research, she identified behaviors of people who fit her definition of true belonging:

- They do not hide their beliefs. They stay connected to current events in the world, and to their relationships, and at the same time remain differentiated.[8] When we engage in a healthy way with people who think, look, and act differently from the way we do, it becomes harder to cut them off and harder to dislike them. We begin to lean into one another in new ways.

- They "speak truth to bullshit. Be civil."[9] As clergy, we might say, "Speak the truth with love." What does this have to do with belonging and loneliness? It gets back to living in integrity and with authenticity.

One Sunday morning, I (Mary Kay) watched a young pastor at a large Lutheran church have an encounter with a grouchy man in the congregation. Pastor Stan had told a joke during his sermon. The elderly man, Donald, approached Stan in the narthex after the service. Donald poked Stan in the chest and said with a clenched jaw, "Don't you ever make a joke in the pulpit." I could see that Stan was taken by surprise, but he quickly composed himself, took a breath, and poked Donald back and said, "That was disrespectful." Donald appeared taken aback, as if he hadn't expected the young pastor to stand up for himself. After that encounter, it seemed as though Donald had a new appreciation for Pastor Stan. And rightfully so.

Pastor Stan stood up for himself and spoke truth
to Donald, even though Donald was a longtime
member of the congregation.

- They believe humans are inextricably connected.
We might think this is an easy thing for people of
faith to do. When things are going well, we maintain the sense that a sacred thread runs throughout
humanity, and we can look at a stranger on the
street and feel connected. But when things aren't
going well—when we are having doubts about
our faith, for example—clergy can feel worse off
than the general population. As clergy, we think
we're never to doubt, and when we do, we certainly can't admit that to anyone. So we not only
feel disconnected from others; we further isolate
ourselves.

When this occurs, our recommendation is to
accept the feeling of disconnect, as unsettling as it
might be, rather than trying to suppress or judge
it. You might then choose to confide in a friend,
colleague, coach, or counselor. You'll likely receive
acceptance and support regardless of the status of
your faith life. If your confidant is honest, you
might even hear that as a spiritual leader, they've
had similar feelings at some point too. The reality
is that all of us, including clergy, are similar to most
every other human in having a faith life that ebbs
and flows.

Brown's research revealed that one of the ways to maintain this belief is to *show up* with other humans in community times of great joy and sorrow. Think about widespread crises like the pandemic. We don't need to intimately know the masked person we pass by on the street. Rather, our masks remind us that we are in this together and therefore that we are inextricably connected. Another powerful example is showing up at a vigil for something like the death of George Floyd. Just being with hundreds of strangers experiencing similar grief helps us feel the inextricable connection Brown talks about.

- They have a strong back, soft front, and wild heart.[10] To find true belonging, we need courage (strong back) to be in the wilderness and stand alone. We need a soft front of compassion, vulnerability, and curiosity. And we need a wild heart—the ability to live with paradox, to live in the tension of both/and, to be both vulnerable and courageous at the same time.

To achieve a lasting feeling of true belonging involves work we must engage in for a lifetime. When we feel true belonging and show up in the world in the ways Brown describes, we stand a chance at beginning to build true community.

TRUE COMMUNITY

We hear time and time again that clergy have no place to just be themselves. There are communities all around them and they are part of communities, but they have no real community. In doing research for this book, we have come to realize we readily throw around the term *community* without knowing what it truly means. Psychiatrist M. Scott Peck writes about establishing true community, and even he has difficulty fully capturing the essence. He offers the following wisdom: "If we are going to use the word meaningfully we must restrict it to a group of individuals who have learned how to communicate honestly with each other, whose relationships go deeper than their masks of composure, and who have developed some significant commitment to 'rejoice together, mourn together,' and to 'delight in each other, make others' conditions our own.' But what, then, does such a rare group look like? How does it function? What is a true definition of community?"[11] He goes on to acknowledge that language often falls short in trying to define community but that true communities are places of inclusivity, commitment, and consensus.[12]

We can't help but notice that the words Peck uses, inclusivity, commitment, and consensus, are words clergy and committed church members long to use to describe their congregations, and sometimes they *do* make that claim. But we, your authors, dare say that at best these declarations are aspirational for most congregations. Churches, as much as the rest of our society, fall short of creating true community. Truly inclusive communities, according to Peck, are "always reaching to extend themselves," to check themselves when they want to exclude anyone at all. In a rather convicting statement, he says, "The great enemy of community is exclusivity. Groups that exclude others because they are poor or doubters or divorced or sinners or of some different race or nationality are not communities; they are cliques—actually defensive bastions against community." He goes on to say that such acceptance of differences within a community is because of the deep commitment—a willingness to coexist—and is crucial.[13] Peck goes on to say, "Community, like marriage, requires that we hang in there when the going gets a little rough."[14] For clergy (and for congregations who are really serious about being true communities), having such an inclusive and committed space would contribute to their sense of belonging. (For congregations, we delve into this topic again in part 3 of the book.)

In chapter 3, we talked about the concept of front stage, backstage, and offstage. The backstage is a place where true community could be created and would be beneficial support in the life of clergy. The good news is that Peck is certain any group can create true community, if they only know the rules to heed in order to do so.

SOCIAL SUPPORT NETWORKS

As previously discussed, according to the research on the UCLA Loneliness Scale, people make meaning of their social world at three levels—called "factors" in the research: the personal self, the relational self, and the collective self. Related to true belonging and true community, the third factor in the scale deals with feelings of group identification; that is, we define ourselves, in part, through groups that provide a sense of identity and belonging.

It appears that having a social support network in one's later years is especially important. In a 2018 study, University of California, San Francisco, researcher Julene Johnson found that joining a choir can combat feelings of loneliness in older adults.[15] In another study, the University of Queensland found that retirees who lose their connection to social groups experience a 10 percent drop in their quality of life for every group membership lost.[16] Humans need others in their lives who value them, whom they can trust, and with whom they can "do life." How many people are needed may vary with each person, but there is little doubt that a social support network is important to almost everyone.

While having a social support network is important to abate feelings of loneliness, simply increasing our number of acquaintances isn't enough. (Recall our earlier discussion about one person feeling lonely in a crowd, while another person feels perfectly fulfilled by themselves.) In addition to increasing the number of social connections, we must also adjust our perceptions about loneliness and make the effort to deepen our relationships so that the *quality* of our interactions improves.

Having said that, a social network does remain an important component of well-being for clergy. Matt Bloom, in his longitudinal study on clergy well-being, indicates four kinds of social relationships that create what he calls an ecosystem of well-being:[17]

- *Significant others* are family and friends with whom one has deep relationship. Bloom goes so far as to say they "meet the powerful need we all have for unconditional positive regard, to be loved as we are and for who we are. Many researchers believe that this is the single most important kind of social support."[18]
- *Similar others* are people in similar roles who understand yours. (This is the backstage.) They understand what it's like to walk in your shoes. Recall the pastor diagnosed with lymphoma. She wanted a clergy support group because the similar others in this ideal group would understand her unique situation. She couldn't find that group.
- *Church* consists of members of the context in which the clergy serves. Having previously made the case for clear, firm relationship boundaries between clergy and their congregations, here

we see others identifying the same people as an important part of our social support. The truth is, we are with these people frequently, sometimes more than with the significant others in our lives, so we need to be in some sort of relationship with them. Bloom suggests that congregations create "mutually responsive relationships, in which each member effectively strives to understand, accept, and care for other members."[19] After all, isn't this what it means to love thy neighbor? The clergy-congregation boundary begins to be crossed when clergy get their needs met from congregation members.

• When *denominational leaders* focus on the well-being of the clergy for whom they are charged to care, clergy feel loved and supported. This focus can take many forms: providing opportunities for connecting and education, simply checking in, and definitely being there for clergy in their times of need. We discuss more about what denominational leaders can do in chapter 9.

When we meet with clergy, we'll often ask them about the quality of their friendships outside of their congregational systems. While most recognize the benefits of such relationships and even express a desire for them, many have let these friendships slide over the years. To drive home the importance of maintaining relationships outside of their clergy role, we'll further ask who their pastor is. Sometimes they can identify someone immediately. Sometimes, they are surprised by the question, which invites them to reflect and hopefully find an answer.

REFLECTIVE SUPERVISION

Having clergy identify who their pastor is can lead to a positive step: actually being in relationship with that person the way their parishioners rely on them. Another important relationship is one of reflective supervision. When we think of the word "supervision," we often think about the oversight a head of staff, executive team, or personnel committee has over a minister's day-in and day-out role in their work context. But there's another type of supervision. The type of supervision we put forth here is provided by a third party (someone who has no formal supervisory oversight into your "employment") who offers you the opportunity to reflect on life in ministry. We call this "reflective supervision." This supervision relationship is a sacred, confidential, and safe place to bring all the joys and concerns of ministry to one who will hold them all with you and guide you to reflect on them.

Author Jane Leach's book *A Charge to Keep: Reflective Supervision and the Renewal of Christian Leadership* describes reflective supervision and the experience of initiating a reflective supervision program in the United Kingdom's Methodist Church. She describes the role of the trained supervisor: "to create intentional space for the exploration of the significant ministry issues that arise within the framework of the expectations, beliefs, and priorities that shape the supervisee's context and work . . . to find the parts of ourselves that can get lost or submerged in the work."[20]

Most clergy don't have this type of formal relationship, but in the United Kingdom, the Methodist church is learning that it's a critical addition to a minister's support system. In the United Kingdom, every Methodist minister has a reflective supervisor who has been trained to provide this sacred space for clergy to reflect on their ministry in ways they don't do anywhere else. At LeaderWise, we've begun to provide reflective supervision, first through a pilot in the United Methodist Church (UMC) in the United States and now for anyone who wants to have this kind of support system.

The program in the United Kingdom began after discerning that clergy in the Methodist Church of Britain (MCB) needed extra support. Subsequently, a pilot program showed that pastors under supervision with a trained third-party supervisor expressed an increase in well-being and a decrease in the experience of isolation (among other things).

The model of supervision that's been implemented in the MCB, and is now being piloted in the UMC in the United States, recognizes three types of topics that clergy bring to the supervisory space:

- *Formative* topics are formational in nature—for example, reflection on one's gifts, skills, and development areas.

- *Restorative* topics attend to the emotional health and well-being of the supervisee.
- *Normative* topics attend to the practices and norms within the ministry context. Here, boundary issues or expectations of the role might be discussed.

In her book, Leach reflects on the necessity of such a third-party supervisory relationship: "Clergy well-being had already become a significant concern with the British church. . . . Without good pastoral support the demands of ministerial practice are likely to lead to burnout, inattention to boundaries, and a lack of focus on the patterns of ministry and church life that support the deep purposes of God."[21] In fact, at Leader-Wise, we have seen this exact prediction play out.

Leach goes on to share the reported positive impacts of reflective supervision through the eighteen-month pilot study. Among them, clergy report they

- felt they had a safe place to discuss and unravel all that's entailed in ministry,
- experienced an increase in confidence in their ability to step into ministry, and
- understood better how they were showing up in ministry and were able to make different choices.[22]

Leach further says that there was "also evidence of an increased sense of belonging through the support of prayer and through the gift of time."[23]

All this is to say that the pastoral supervision relationship is a critical part of clergy's social and backstage support structure. In this sacred space between a clergyperson, their supervisor, and God, a minister can come home to themselves and to God and be renewed to go back out into ministry once again, ready for the journey, all the while knowing that someone knows and cares about them deeply.

We take up this topic again in chapter 10, where we encourage denominations and judicatories to make reflective supervision a part of the support structure for their clergy. But know that you don't need to wait for your denomination to require this support. Like coaching or spiritual direction, you can seek it on your own, as some clergy have already done.

WISDOM FROM OTHER CLERGY

In our research on loneliness at LeaderWise, we asked clergy for their own wisdom about how they find, or imagine finding, belonging. As you read through these responses, first focus on one or two, calling to mind the broaden-and-build theory of positive psychology. You can create an upward spiral of positive emotions by starting with any one of these. Here's a summary of what we heard:

- Fifty-seven percent of respondents suggested that *enhancing their social support network* would lead to a greater sense of belonging. Specifically, they

suggested building, connecting, enhancing, and
maintaining
- family relationships (spouse, partner, children in
  various activities)
- existing friendships (inside/outside the church
  context)
- denominational supports (discussions with eccle-
  siastical supervisors/personnel)
- other existing social supports (clergy mentorship,
  coaching, counseling)
- Thirty-one percent of respondents desired
  increased opportunities for social interaction. They
  indicated the importance of enlarging the number and types of opportunities to develop quality
  relationships:
  - family (new activities for interacting with
    spouse, partner, children in various activities)
  - clergy/peers/colleagues (joining networking
    groups, clergy learning or support groups)
  - new relationships (developing new friendships,
    joining book clubs, recreational leagues, com-
    munity theaters)
  - denominational programs (request denomina-
    tions to develop programs/resources/assistance
    for those who are lonely)
- Fifteen percent of respondents reflected that
  improving social skills would be worthwhile.
  They focused on the importance of developing

interpersonal communication skills. These clergy recommended

- ○ professional assistance (psychotherapist, job coach, spiritual advisor)
- ○ formal education/training (loneliness workshop, social skills training)
- ○ other activities (social role-play, homework)
- Fourteen percent of respondents recognized the need to *do more self-care*—that is, to strengthen one's resilience by taking action to preserve or improve one's own general health and well-being—through
  - ○ individual activities (hobbies, physical exercise, nutrition, pets)
  - ○ spiritual activities (meditation, Sabbath, exercising faith)
  - ○ other self-care activities
- Seven percent of respondents recognized the *cognitive distortions* that we're prone to have when feeling lonely and offered ways of addressing them to improve psychological well-being, including
  - ○ developing realistic thoughts about the clergy profession (loneliness as part of the job, the commonality of the experience)
  - ○ developing realistic thoughts about the self (loneliness does not represent personal failure, the need to renew commitment to personal mission/goals/purposes)

- exercising one's power/agency (develop plans to deal with loneliness, act in spite of anxiety or fear)
- seeking input from a counselor to learn how to identify and reframe cognitive distortions (e.g., "It may be challenging, but I can learn how to have time for both ministry and friends," "Just because some people say they don't want to date a minister, there are lots of people who would")

The input of our clergy generally aligns with the broader research that emphasizes the importance of social relationships. Specifically, the recommended actions—enhancing social support networks, increasing opportunities for social interaction, and improving social skills—are proven ways to decrease social isolation and loneliness. At the same time, we encourage clergy to consider more carefully the benefits of cognitive strategies, such as observing and reframing thoughts. Of all the interventions, the research finds this approach consistently helps people find greater peace of mind, no matter their situation.

FOR REFLECTION AND DISCUSSION

1. This chapter discussed true belonging and true community. What struck you about those

concepts? Have you ever experienced what you would call true belonging or true community?

2. Do you have a backstage support system? If not, how might you create one?

3. What concept resonated most with you in this chapter? Why?

6

The Spirituality Connection

Know thyself.

—Socrates

Very early in the morning, while it was still dark, Jesus got up,
left the house and went off to a solitary place, where he prayed.

—Mark 1:35 NIV

One can be lonely and not be tossed away by it.

—Katagiri Roshi, Zen master

Spirituality does not require religious faith but is characterized by humility and ever-present connectedness to oneself or
to others or to an entity that is transcendent, such as Mother
Nature or God or the soul. It helps reduce stress in many people
and allows them to be more at peace, happier and healthier. . . .
Feeling connected to something makes you feel less lonely.[1]

—Michelle Brubaker, "Is Spirituality a Component of Wisdom?"

Every five years on a milestone birthday, I (Mark) engage in an activity to mark the occasion. For the first event, at age forty, I climbed a mountain with a friend, and five years later I rode with ten thousand other bicyclists in the RAGBRAI, a weeklong party on wheels across Iowa. The last three milestone birthdays, I've turned inward, participating in ten-day silent retreats. The first was a Buddhist retreat with Thich Nhat Hanh, a Zen master, in Colorado. Alone with my thoughts for most of each day, I discovered seeds of shame and self-judgment, and learned the practice of mindfulness and self-compassion. Five years later, I meditated with Buddhist monastics in Mississippi. Nothing notable happened, which can be part of the spiritual life too. In fact, I was a bit bored. On the most recent retreat, in the mountains of New Mexico, my mind and spirit were receptive, and it was life transforming. As I wrestled with the demons of my past and present, as well as fears of the future, I found my psychological defenses crumbling. After a particularly unsettling meditation session in which my mind was in overdrive, I walked through a mountain meadow and wept. I realized I was utterly alone, and to my mind, everyone who had loved me unconditionally was now dead. I also was acutely aware of my own aging and mortality. That night I had a fitful sleep, even talking with dead relatives.

The next dawn, though, I woke up with a preternatural calm. A transformation had taken place in the wee hours. I woke up with a deep assurance that those who loved me were still with me. They were simultaneously gone yet present. I had also long struggled with the tension between my Christian heritage, my role as a Christian minister, and Buddhist spiritual practices, and suddenly there was no conflict. A message came to me: "All creatures just want to be enlightened," whatever the path. The final revelation stays with me to this day and guides my life because an inner voice said to me, "There is a benevolent force in the universe that loves you and knows you by name." My life has never been the same.

FOR REFLECTION

- With which part of this story do you resonate?
- What spiritual practices help you feel loved and grounded?

Before joining LeaderWise, I (Mary Kay) served as synod minister in the Evangelical Lutheran Church in America. One spring, the whole synod office staff team met with a spiritual director for a retreat. In that session, he asked us when we engaged in our private spiritual practices. To a person, our answers encompassed times that were outside the typical workday for a synod staff person. His response to us was something like "Your synod needs you to be healthy, and your spiritual practice is one of the components that help you be healthy, so it's part of your job. Stop doing it outside of your job as if it's extra or not critical."

We readily recognized the spiritual director was right. We do need a spiritual connection and spiritual practices to be part of our overall well-being plan, and our congregations and denominations benefit from our being healthy too. That conversation gave us permission to begin taking time during our workday to find our connection to the Divine. It also gave us permission to hold one another accountable to that same thing.

That conversation also made us realize that many clergy "do spirituality" as part of their preparation for Sunday morning—as more of a professional activity than a personal one. While we agree that we should be able to attend to our spiritual connection to the Divine at any hour of the day, without feeling guilty that we are "on the clock," we don't want clergy to confuse the preparation for Sunday morning and the attention to their own well-being. That distinction needs to be kept well within its boundaries.

Fortuitously, regular practices of connecting with the Divine can curb feelings of loneliness. The term *practices* means there are *behaviors*—actions—attached to them. Sometimes spiritual practices are also called "disciplines." To us, a "discipline" connotes more of a way of life as opposed to a behavior that's invoked momentarily, even if often. We think of the following activities as both practices and disciplines—both behaviors and ways of life. We begin with solitude as a spiritual practice.

SOLITUDE AS A SPIRITUAL PRACTICE

A few times in the Gospel stories of the Bible, we hear that Jesus tried to go to a quiet place by himself to pray. It seems he doesn't get a chance to stay in these quiet places very long before his disciples or the crowds find him. Only a couple times in the New Testament do we get a hint of the emotion Jesus is feeling. The rest of the time, we have no idea how Jesus is faring. And yet we can imagine ministry was demanding for Jesus, with little chance to silence the world and just be. Ministry was challenging then, just as it is for ministers in our day. With so many pressures, we can imagine Jesus sometimes felt alone, even though he was almost always with others. And he chose—he *needed*—solitude.

Henri Nouwen observed that loneliness is part of our human condition, so we may feel lonely at times. Nouwen also believed that aloneness, solitude, is part of our spiritual life and essential to spiritual growth. Our task is to make a cognitive shift (see chapter 4)—to walk the difficult road of conversion—from loneliness to solitude. Nouwen elaborates, "Instead of running away from our loneliness and trying to forget or deny it, we have to protect it and turn it into a fruitful solitude. To live a spiritual life we must first find the courage to enter into the desert of our loneliness and to change it by gentle and persistent efforts into a garden of solitude. . . . The movement from loneliness to solitude, however, is the beginning of any spiritual life because it is the movement from the restless senses to the restful spirit."[2]

Earlier in the book, we shared with you that Vivek Murthy, during his tenure as the nineteenth surgeon general of the United States, declared loneliness an epidemic. In *Together*, he distinguishes between loneliness and solitude. He says, "When we feel lonely, we're unhappy and long to escape this emotional pain." He goes on, "Solitude, by contrast, is a state of peaceful aloneness or voluntary isolation. It is an opportunity for self-reflection and a chance to connect with ourselves without distraction or disturbance. . . . Developing comfort with solitude, then, is an essential part of strengthening our connection to ourselves and by extension enabling our connection with others. Solitude, paradoxically, protects against loneliness."[3]

As a spiritual practice, solitude is a chosen companion, teacher, and healer. In our busy society, though, where action is key and we don't know who we are without comparing ourselves to another, solitude can feel foreign to most or downright scary to some. We live in a society that is busy and noisy and filled with distractions of all sorts. We don't have much downtime. Especially in the United States, we have a tendency to address problems through action, making the results of our work the criteria of success and of our very identity.[4] We also face daily the subtle message that if we don't have people to be with, then we must not be worthy ourselves. So we get busy (even if it's with busywork), and we stay connected (even if only superficially).

The truth is, in our networked, success-driven world, we have lost the ability to *just be* with ourselves. We'd do anything to avoid being alone, and we panic when we have nothing to fill every moment. Intentional solitude quiets the world around us to create space for reflection and for just being. *Being* precedes *doing*. Contemplation precedes action.

My (Mary Kay's) husband once read in a book, "Solitude is man's best friend." (Sorry about the gendered language. It's verbatim.) That simple sentence meant so much to him that he wrote it on a scrappy piece of faded paper and posted it to the plywood wall in our old primitive, tiny cabin (that we lovingly call "the shack") that sits on a granite knoll above a small lake. This is our "happy place." It is a place where solitude comes easily, and I seek it as my refuge.

It doesn't seem like many such spaces exist anymore. Even in a pandemic, when we're staying home and apart from others, we lack the opportunity for true solitude. Distractions—cell phones, email, and social media—are constantly calling to us, some of them presenting others' curated lives, which appear to be busy, happy, and full, contributing to our belief that we lead lonely lives. Even owning a cabin, a retreat, I can escape to, it isn't easy for me to disconnect, to take time away for just me, or just me and my husband, or just me and God.

Even so, as I rest in the middle of a vast forest that contains immeasurably big old-growth white pine trees, alongside a beautiful lake, solitude beckons like a best friend. During one extended stay at our retreat years ago, I went into town for supplies and received the news that my friend and colleague Pastor Sarah had passed away suddenly. In a state of shock, I headed for the trails on our property—trails that would take me to the base of one of the huge white pines that our Anishinaabe siblings call *Nokomis*, or "grandmother." There, I sat at the base of the great tree, and it held me as the reality of the news sunk in. Solitude was a comforter and a guide to and through grief.

Solitude is a space for far more than grief, however. Solitude helps us reset our lives on emotional, physical, mental, and spiritual levels. And paradoxical as it may sound, solitude is a soothing balm for loneliness. Henri Nouwen, in *Out of Solitude*, calls solitude a lonely place—but not in a negative sense. He says, "Somewhere we know that without a lonely place our lives are in danger. Somewhere we know that without silence, words lose their meaning, that without listening, speaking no longer heals, that without distance closeness cannot cure."[5] Deep down, our souls know they need solitude; perhaps they cry for it.

While intentional solitude is one of the best ways to get in touch with your soul, choosing *only* solitude can be a warning sign that something is out of balance. We choose solitude so that we can then engage more deeply, and in a healthier way, with society. We choose solitude so that we can reconnect with ourselves, with the earth, with the Source of our being. That reconnection reminds us that we are beloved just as we are, that we are enough. When we can get to *that* place, then we can reengage with the world with the health and freedom to offer ourselves and our ministry in a fresh and satisfying way—without the self-talk that questions every move we make, that says we are not good enough or an imposter. When we reconnect with ourselves and the Source of our being, we regain the capacity to sit with others in their brokenness and pain without needing to say the right thing and without the desire to run away. Psychotherapist and former monk Thomas Moore wrote, in the foreword to Nouwen's *Out of Solitude*, about what he calls "ordinary mysticism." He says it is the "capacity in each of us to find the stillness in ourselves, and in life that is the most productive place of all. The paradox is that we are most connected and most creative while living in that special kind of solitude."[6]

If that isn't enough, here's a bit more incentive to seek solitude. Research has shown that among the benefits of solitude are increased creativity, deeper spiritual connection, and paradoxically, an increase in feelings of intimacy.[7] Solitude strengthens our sense of identity by giving us the space to connect with ourselves and to reflect on the loved ones in our lives.

You don't have to buy twenty acres in the middle of a national forest to experience solitude. And you don't have to go on a ten-day silent retreat every year either. You do need to remove the distractions that get in the way of being with yourself uninterrupted so you can tune into your deepest feelings, thereby getting to know yourself over and over again.

Solitude can happen in many ways and in varying amounts of time. One minister, for instance, adheres to daily, weekly, monthly, and yearly rhythms for Sabbath keeping. We would say the same rhythm is also necessary for solitude (perhaps Sabbath and solitude are two sides of the same coin). What does solitude in a moment look like? It's stepping away from your desk and going to a place apart, a place to attend to your soul for just a few minutes. Perhaps your solitude place is your garden or a chair that is especially comfortable. In that place, you can take some deep breaths, declutter your mind, recenter yourself, and pray or meditate. Daily, maybe it is a ten-minute morning meditation practice. On a weekly basis, perhaps you take a long, silent walk or go sit on a park bench with only your deepest thoughts for an hour or two. Each month, you might plan to get away for a whole day to do the same. Those who embrace the Buddhist tradition talk about regularly taking a day of mindfulness as an essential component of maintaining one's meditative and spiritual practices. Every year, you might consider a weeklong retreat or study leave. Ultimately, you must find what works for you.

It may feel a bit paradoxical that to combat loneliness we need times of solitude. Unless we can check in and connect with ourselves, however, we don't stand a chance to be able to do the same with others.

In a blessing by John O'Donohue, called "For Solitude," he writes, "May you learn to see yourself with the same delight, pride, and expectation with which God sees you in every moment."[8] When we can find our connection to the Divine through solitude, then we come to realize we are beloved children of God—and we are never alone.

GRATITUDE AS A SPIRITUAL PRACTICE

In this moment, I (Mary Kay) am sitting at my cabin in front of a large picture window that overlooks the forest and our small lake. Most days right now, the bugs are bad, so I can't spend a lot of time outside—at least not without lots of extra clothing and smelly repellent. I am so grateful for the beauty of this sanctuary in my life, its solitude, the wild raspberries and blueberries that will soon be ready to pick (and the bees that are working hard to make that happen). And I know how privileged I am to have all of this. I don't deserve it, which makes me grateful all over again that I have it. During really stressful and hard times in my life, this has been a place of refuge, one for which I have felt gratitude even in the midst of suffering.

In reviewing the literature on gratitude, we're struck by how often ancient spiritual practices are now being validated by contemporary science as promoting psychological health. Many practices can be viewed as completely secular in nature and have been studied scientifically, and yet most spiritual people (regardless of religion) would call them spiritual practices. Gratitude and meditation are two of these practices.

For example, some research studies have discovered a correlation between the practice of gratitude and increased feelings of social connectedness and subjective well-being.[9] The authors of one study identified how this unfolds: "[The] positive emotion of gratefulness helps build the social and cognitive resources in terms of social connectedness and presence of meaning in life, which are effective in increasing subjective well being."[10] It appears that one builds upon the other, demonstrating the broaden-and-build theory that we introduced in our introduction to part 2.[11] Gratitude broadens our attention, thoughts, and behaviors in a constructive way. Over time, this thought-action cycle of positive emotions, which begins with gratitude, builds our social and cognitive resources, enabling us to cope with subsequent stressful encounters. In other words, an increase in gratitude leads to a sense of purpose and social connectedness, and ultimately, these contribute to an overall increase in subjective well-being. Other studies have specifically linked the practice of gratitude to fewer feelings of loneliness.[12]

We're also reminded of the apostle Paul in his letter to the Philippians. He said, "I thank my God every time I remember you, constantly praying with joy in every one of my prayers for all of you" (Phil 1:3–4). Paul wrote this letter from prison. It couldn't have been a very joyous time, and yet he used the word "joy" as he penned thoughts to the people of Philippi. How can a person unjustly imprisoned feel any joy at all? As Brother David Steindl-Rast points out, "The root of joy is gratefulness. . . . It is not joy that makes us grateful; it is gratitude that makes us joyful."[13] Paul gives thanks every time he remembers the beloved people of Philippi. He is tapping into the spiritual practice of gratitude—"constantly praying with joy in every one of my prayers." There's always something for which to be grateful, and when we pause and reflect on that, we see the world and our circumstances in a new and better way. We are shoring ourselves up. With a little practice, gratitude can become a way of life, and it can make meaning out of what otherwise might feel like hopelessness.

Many of us are familiar with the practice of keeping a gratitude journal or acknowledging daily that for which we are grateful. At one of our workshops, Debbie, a participant, enthusiastically related the way she has combined the wholesome effects of counting her blessings with connecting with friends. She has a group of friends with whom she has an ongoing text chain that connects them daily, and in these texts, they regularly share moments of blessing and gratitude. As Debbie commented, "It helps us to remember that even when life is hard there is much to be thankful for."

At our retreats, we often introduce participants to the practice of gratitude walking. Picture a group of twenty-five to thirty individuals walking deliberately and mindfully through the grounds and becoming absorbed in the beauty around them. Without prompting, many will take out their smartphones and begin to snap pictures of trees, flowers, rocks, logs, and other everyday wonders. When we reconvene, people are often eager to share their discoveries and savor the moment. All of this comes from just slowing down and noticing.

We invite you to take a gratitude walk.[14] Don your favorite walking shoes and stroll through the streets of your neighborhood. Notice all the beauty and goodness around you, and send silent prayers to God and the universe. If you encounter people, smile at them, being grateful for their presence on this earth. Not only is the act of noticing important, but also by walking, you are getting exercise and increasing your oxygen intake, so you'll just feel better. Finally, studies have shown that the mere act of smiling at a stranger increases a sense of connection.[15] All of these activities will make you feel more connected to the Divine and the world. Based on our experience, we can assure you that you will begin to feel better and less lonely.

By no means are we suggesting that you fake positive feelings. Rather, even in the midst of whatever feelings are true for you, you can acknowledge that for which you are grateful too. Perhaps especially in difficult or stressful times, we can experience the power of gratitude—feeling a little lift in our spirit when moments before, circumstances felt pretty hopeless.

WORSHIP

In yet another clergy-must-have-it-made vein, communal experiences with rituals bring about feelings of connectedness and belonging. So if you're not clergy, consider a return to your faith community. And if you're clergy? We're preaching to the choir when we say that the worship you are leading doesn't count. You know you are not able to truly worship when your role is to ensure those in the pews and online have an experience of the Divine.

Clergy need to find separate places to reconnect with God in worship. That may feel impossible, perhaps due to your location or schedule and life obligations, so this might not be your path to belonging. (Don't forget that doing any of the number of things we've suggested will set you solidly on that path to belonging.) And yet if you've longed for a worship experience just for you, maybe it's time for you to reach out to other clergy in your neighborhood (no matter their denomination!) and start a Sunday evening house church or similar activity.

THE MIDDLE WAY

Faith traditions have much to say on the topic of loneliness, if you take the time to look. The Buddhist tradition talks about "cool loneliness" and "hot loneliness." The latter is the all-consuming and overwhelming feeling of loneliness. Cool loneliness is manageable and can even lead to enlightenment. In this tradition, the way to deal with loneliness is through practicing presence (mindfulness, as we've already discussed) and meditation. The goal is to "step into a world of no reference point without polarizing or solidifying. This is called the middle way, or the sacred path of the warrior."[16]

Pema Chödrön, a Buddhist nun, talks about the middle way. She says, "When you wake up in the morning and out of nowhere comes the heartache of alienation and loneliness, could you use that as a golden opportunity? Rather than persecuting yourself or feeling that something terribly wrong is happening, right there in the moment of sadness and longing, could you relax and touch the limitless space of the human heart?"[17]

Chödrön offers six aspects of cool loneliness. The goal is to move from what feels like hot loneliness into something that feels more like cool loneliness:

- Less desire—the willingness to be lonely without resolution. Chödrön says, "So even if the hot loneliness is there, and for 1.6 seconds we sit with that restlessness when yesterday we couldn't sit for even one . . . that's the path of bravery."
- Contentment—accepting that overcoming loneliness will likely not bring lasting joy and rather being content with whatever is happening in the moment.
- Avoiding unnecessary activities. When we feel hot loneliness, our human tendency is to act our way out of it and to do something. We might call it numbing. We keep ourselves busy so we don't have to feel the pain. Chödrön, alternatively, asks, "Could we stop trying to escape from being alone with ourselves? What about practicing not jumping and grabbing when we panic? Could we just settle down and have some compassion and respect for ourselves?"
- Complete discipline—being willing to just sit and be alone with whatever is going on. In these

moments, we look to loneliness to be a teacher of living with the unresolved issues in our lives.

- Not wandering in the world of desire. The world of desire is where we look for alternatives, things to satisfy us: "Not wandering in the world of desire is about relating directly with how things are. Loneliness is not a problem. Loneliness is nothing to be solved. The same thing is true for any other experience we might have."

- Not seeking security from one's discursive thoughts. In meditation, our "thinking" is transparent and ungraspable: "We're encouraged to just touch that chatter and let it go, not make much ado about nothing."[18]

If your loneliness feels "hot" or severe, perhaps try one of Chödrön's techniques to cool it off a bit so that it's manageable. You might even learn something from it.

LOVINGKINDNESS

Also part of the middle way, meditation changes our perspective on loneliness. A specific practice of meditation is called "lovingkindness." In lovingkindness meditation, we begin in a relaxed frame of mind, perhaps seated or walking mindfully, and focus on repeating a series of phrases timed to our in-breath and out-breath. While we do so, we are consciously opening our hearts. A common series of phrases is "May I be filled with lovingkindness," "May I be safe from inner and outer dangers," "May I be well in body and mind," "May I be at ease and happy." After saying it for ourselves, we next say it for those we love: "May you be filled with lovingkindness," "May you be safe from inner and outer dangers," "May you be well in body and mind," "May you be at ease and happy." We then focus on others for whom we have neutral feelings (e.g., a clerk at the store where we buy groceries), and we finish by sending lovingkindness to those with whom we are in conflict or dislike.

In a study on lovingkindness meditation, researchers found that even just a few minutes of lovingkindness meditation increased feelings of social connectedness.[19] Jack Kornfield, a renowned American Buddhist teacher, explains, "Lovingkindness can be practiced anywhere. You can use this meditation in traffic jams, in buses, and on airplanes. As you silently practice this meditation among people, you will come to feel a wonderful connection with them—the power of lovingkindness. It will calm your mind and keep you connected to your heart."[20]

In Buddhism, our approach to meditation is no striving, no grasping, and no judgment. We accept our experience of meditation—as well as the world—as it is. Like any spiritual practice, our ability to benefit from it may occur over time as we practice, though if we enter with the idea of gaining something from it, then we may miss the opportunity to grow from it. Paradoxically, when we practice without a goal, that's when we may see positive changes in our life. If practicing meditation has felt frustrating to you in the past, start small. Begin with sitting for just a few minutes, and give yourself a lot of grace in the process—accepting whatever comes. Over time, this practice of acceptance and equanimity of mind will likely transfer to other parts of your life too.

It's easy to think that because clergy are in "the business" of spirituality and religion, we wouldn't need to talk about it so much here. However, our own connection to the Divine can get lost in the day-to-day of making sure our "job gets done." So we hope this chapter has been a helpful reminder of perhaps why you felt called to ministry in the first place—out of a sense of deep connection to something greater than yourself—and that if you feel as though you've lost that, you can find it again. You will be a better minister, and you will feel less lonely!

FOR REFLECTION AND DISCUSSION

1. What has your experience with spiritual practice been over the course of your ministry?
2. How has it differed from season to season?
3. What spiritual practice do you feel called to in this season?

Being Wise about Loneliness

As in life, chill for best results.

—Slogan, Sparkling Ice water

Teri is pastor of a 150-member congregation in a midsize northeastern town. Although the state recently mandated policies that limit public gatherings to thirty people and that require people to wear masks, Teri finds that many towns-people, including congregation members, simply ignore the mandates. After having met online for several months, there appears to be a groundswell in the congregation to resume in-person meetings and worship services. Teri is nervous about her personal health and the health of her spouse (who has underlying health concerns) and children. In addition, she worries about the well-being of older adults in her congregation, since they would likely comprise the majority of people returning for in-person events.

At a recent church council meeting, there was a heated debate. Those in favor of reopening in-person events cited (1) concerns about finances—and even survival of the congregation—if the congregation continues to gather only online (will people fall out of "the church habit"?) and (2) the emotional well-being of older adults. On the other side, in almost equal numbers, were those who support restrictions and continuing online. They pointed out (1) the risk to the physical health of church members, church staff, and the pastor and (2) the general disregard in their community for rules about masks, social distancing, and size of gatherings—and the consequent risk of infecting others. Teri feels at wit's end. If she advocates for what she truly believes, she will likely alienate a sizable portion of the congregation, and if she doesn't, she risks the health of vulnerable individuals, including her spouse and children.

FOR REFLECTION

- To what part of Teri's story do you relate?
- How do you typically wrestle with complicated issues that aren't cut-and-dried?

We live in a highly polarized time, and ministry often places clergy at the center of competing worldviews and value systems. To act skillfully as we navigate these tensions is a challenge, and we often feel lonely and isolated when we disappoint or upset people—even though there is no way to avoid it, given the division on many issues. In our work with clergy, we've found the research literature on wisdom, which discusses models for making wise decisions, to be useful in this time of complex decision-making. You may wonder, though, why discuss wisdom in a book about loneliness? Interestingly enough, research in recent years has shown that wisdom is an antidote to loneliness. Studies have demonstrated a negative correlation between the two. That is, wise people don't tend to score high on the loneliness scale, and conversely, people who score high on loneliness don't tend to score high on wisdom scales. Just as loneliness is associated with a lack of well-being, wisdom is associated with higher levels of well-being. The research further reveals that the exercise of wisdom, at its best, fosters deeper relationships and community bonds.

THE WISE REASONING MODEL

At LeaderWise, we draw on a couple models of wisdom, and one we find particularly useful on a day-to-day basis is the *wise reasoning model*.[1] The model assumes that wisdom can be learned and practiced, and it offers four aspects to arriving at wise decisions. It begins with *intellectual humility*. Many decisions don't require that we exercise wisdom, as there is a straightforward answer. We draw on wisdom when a problem has multiple levels of complexity that require an attitude of intellectual humility to appreciate the limits of our knowledge and abilities. We also need to acknowledge the truth of the second point of the model, *impermanence.* What has worked in the past may not be the right approach today. The final two points connect us to the social aspect of wise leadership: *seeking the perspectives of others* and *integrating these perspectives* into our thinking to arrive at a wise decision.

We find these last two aspects can take the edge off the loneliness that many clergy experience. The church world is rapidly changing, and it's too heavy a burden for any one of us to carry the weight of organizational decisions alone. At LeaderWise, in our decision-making, we emphasize shared leadership and regularly solicit the input and feedback of other team members. By sharing the responsibility, we feel more connected and less lonely and isolated, and we arrive at better decisions. Clergy can use the wise reasoning model by

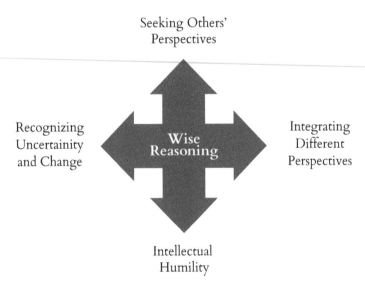

Seeking Others'
Perspectives

Recognizing
Uncertainity
and Change

Wise
Reasoning

Integrating
Different
Perspectives

Intellectual
Humility

Figure 7.1. Wise reasoning

thinking through difficult challenges with the help of either parishioners or colleagues, as many of the problems in one setting are similar to those in another. Being humble and seeking the input of others will often validate our experience and build camaraderie, which can decrease our loneliness and bolster our well-being.

Dilip V. Jeste, who studies wisdom and loneliness at the University of California at San Diego, offers another helpful model. With Scott LaFee, he has coauthored the book *Wiser: The Scientific Roots of Wisdom, Compassion, and What Makes Us Good*. Based on Jeste's research, they outline seven components to wisdom:

1. Pro-social behavior (empathy/compassion/altruism)
2. Emotional regulation (ability to maintain control over emotions regardless of the situation)
3. Self-reflection
4. Acceptance of uncertainty and diversity of perspectives
5. The ability to be decisive (in the midst of those uncertainties and diversity of perspectives)
6. The ability to give appropriate advice and support to others
7. Spirituality[2]

Reviewing Jeste's work, another writer comments, "Wisdom, say the researchers, includes an ability to be reflective and thoughtful about any experience. It also includes an ability to step back and see things not as simply about ourselves, but as about a context and a situation. And finally, it involves a capacity to see things as complex, multi-faceted, and often contradictory, and to find ways to manage these contradictions with some degree of flexibility."[3]

Interested in how wise the research would say you are? One thing you can do today is take the Jeste-Thomas Wisdom Index assessment.[4] You'll receive feedback on how you score for each dimension as well as an overall wisdom score. As indicated, the good news is that wisdom can be learned and developed, so you can celebrate your strong scores and pinpoint areas for improvement.

Jeste's research further suggests how wisdom might serve as an antidote to loneliness. Let's take a look at the seven characteristics of wisdom and overlay them with our discussions on loneliness. First, we would place the first three characteristics on Jeste's list in the category of emotional intelligence (sometimes called EQ). People with a high EQ can move beyond their emotions and don't allow them to hijack their prefrontal cortex (the higher reasoning part of the brain), which enables them to evaluate situations in a more objective manner. When we feel isolated or lonely, these wisdom characteristics can help us reevaluate our initial emotional reaction, normalize our experience, and problem solve.

Second, acceptance of uncertainty and diversity of opinions (fourth on the list) and the ability to be decisive amid them (fifth on the list) allow us to still function well when we encounter unsettling situations, including experiences of isolation and feelings of loneliness. Rather than feeling paralyzed by our emotions, we are able to make a decision and take one step forward, breaking the gridlock in our brains.

Third, the simple act of giving support to others stops loneliness in its tracks because we feel more connected to others—that inextricable human connection Brené Brown talks about.

Other research has demonstrated steps we can take to learn, practice, and develop wisdom.[5] While the research literature is vast, here are some techniques we've found particularly helpful in our work.

SELF-AWARENESS

Wisdom begins with self-awareness. In the wise reasoning model, we start by humbly recognizing our limitations, which prompts us to seek out the input and support of others. Remaining aware of styles of thinking that can sabotage our efforts to act wisely is also helpful. Robert Sternberg, a leading researcher of wisdom, wrote an intriguing article, "Why Smart People Can Be So Foolish," in which he identifies five fallacies—or thinking errors—that trip us up and interfere with wise decision-making:

- Unrealistic optimism. Because we've thought about an issue more than others, we can discount certain risks, dismiss the concerns of others, and trust that things will just work out.
- Egocentrism. We're indispensable as leaders and our organizations couldn't function without us.

- Omniscience. We know all there is to know about a topic.
- Omnipotence. We're all powerful within our organizations and can influence others to get our way.
- Invulnerability. We can do whatever we want with impunity.[6]

In our work with clergy, we've seen these fallacies manifested numerous times in multiple contexts. We've heard some take a hard-line stand on an issue because they know the Scriptures, theology, or their denomination's polity better than their parishioners. We've seen other clergy take unnecessary risks and exercise their power without discretion because they're "cashing in" on their social capital. We've also heard a few wonder, "Who else would they get to be their minister?"—confident that the answer is "No one!" All of these can contribute to interpersonal strain and social alienation, as the ministers are setting themselves up in opposition to the community rather than building relationships and acting in concert with congregation members. These behaviors, even when subtle, can disrupt wise leadership and contribute to a minister's loneliness and social isolation.

Aside from helping us avoid mistakes, self-awareness can help us exercise wisdom too. When we are faced with a decision, it reminds us to slow down, check with others, and bring them on board, even if we're certain of the right approach. Ultimately, this practice will benefit us by building goodwill, solidifying community bonds, and establishing a protocol for decision-making when choices are less clear cut. It can also diminish the feelings of being on the periphery of the communities we serve as clergy.

EGO DECENTERING

In our clergy workshops on wise leadership, we share the practice of ego decentering. Research has shown that it's one of the most effective ways to decrease emotional reactivity and increase objectivity for wise problem-solving in difficult circumstances.[7] It's the practice of mentally taking ourselves out of the center of the situation and observing ourselves as if in the third person (as "he," "she," "they," etc.). When we view ourselves in a situation in the first person ("I," "me") and worry about the possible implications of a decision for ourselves, the stakes can feel high, and we are prone to overreacting. Others may see our response to a situation as defensive or out of proportion. Ego decentering has the benefit of providing us with cognitive distance to slow the pace of our thinking and see things more clearly. Researchers find that we're often far wiser when offering advice to others than in managing our own responses, and ego decentering draws upon that reality by enabling us to step outside of ourselves and provide advice to ourselves.[8] This is one reason journaling often works for people. The dynamic at play is that we become our own internal consultant or coach, who can provide much better insight than if we relied upon our own initial read of a situation.

Rick, a pastor in his early thirties, accepted his first call to a church in the upper Midwest. Having grown up in a different part of the country, he wrestled with the culture of the region, in which people tend to be emotionally reserved. If they were angry with him, they would smile and reassure him rather than acknowledge it openly. Anticipating an upcoming church council meeting, Rick started to worry that people were upset about a recent sermon, though he had heard only indirect comments. He found himself waking up in the middle of the night and having trouble focusing on tasks during the day.

Rick agreed to try two ego-decentering techniques. In the first, he imagined how Jesus would handle ministering to this congregation, especially picturing the way Jesus might respond if people fell silent at the church council meeting instead of talking directly about their concerns. The second technique was to write in his journal as if he were his own coach. He began, "OK, Rick, you're in quite the pickle, because you believe people are upset with you but won't say anything directly to you. They just go silent and freeze you out. Rick, what have you tried?" At this point, Rick recounted in his journal the sequence of events. Then his inner coach returned, and he wrote these words: "Rick, I can see why this is unsettling to you—and I feel for you. I'm curious if you tried naming their silence when it occurs and wondering out loud about what's going on." Rick continued to record his dialogue with his inner coach for another twenty minutes or so.

Although things didn't go perfectly at the church council meeting, as people looked uncomfortable and a long awkward moment ensued when he named the dynamic, a couple of council members eventually opened up enough to acknowledge that his sermon bordered too closely on politics for their liking. At the same time, they recognized that he was still learning about their church. Rick expressed gratitude that they shared their experience with him, and they agreed to serve as a sounding board in the future as he tried to better understand their culture. Mostly, Rick reported that he felt more grounded and less reactive in the meeting due to these techniques, which enabled him to stay emotionally present and connected with the church members despite the tensions in the room.

SHARED WISDOM

Wisdom can ease loneliness by taking the focus off ourselves and concerns about how we'll be perceived in our decision-making. Wisdom further helps because it is a shared enterprise, as we actively seek out and integrate the input of others. Although the research literature in the development of organizational wisdom is just beginning, it suggests that organizations can take conscious steps to become wiser too.[9] As with most leadership models, the movement starts with the leader. Clergy can set the tone for their congregations by learning, practicing, and openly referring to the elements of wise decision-making, almost all of which involve taking the focus off ourselves and integrating multiple viewpoints and opinions. Many congregants will take notice of a minister's humility in the face of complex decisions and their invitation for others to share their perspectives and experiences to arrive at the best decision possible. In fact, creating a culture of humility and shared responsibility is a key step in developing wise organizations.

In our workshops on wisdom, clergy sometimes share that a core group of influential people in their congregations would likely resist a model of wise decision-making due to their own self-interests. This is certainly a possibility. If this is your situation, you can still seek the input of others by consulting with people outside of your organization, such as a coach, counselor, or colleague. Two benefits might ensue: (1) these trusted others can provide different perspectives and approaches in working with a complex situation, and (2) the very act of reaching out can help ease the social isolation and loneliness of taking an unpopular position. The takeaway is that wise leadership is a social act that you can practice and develop. In the process, you will feel more connected to others.

FOR REFLECTION AND DISCUSSION

1. How might you put the wise reasoning model into practice?
2. Which of Jeste's seven components of wisdom are strengths for you? Which would you like to work on?
3. What has been your experience with trying to decenter yourself on an issue in order to gain perspective?

8

Resilience Matters

Pastor Kerry was a resilient leader. Single and new to the community, Kerry asked their judicatory staff for introductions to other single clergy in the area. Then Kerry reached out and introduced themselves and arranged an online text study for the people Kerry was meeting. It started small, with no real commitment, but Kerry, understanding the need for support, kept at being the organizer of the group.

After the group had been together for many months, Kerry was diagnosed with a severe illness with an uncertain outcome. Kerry chose to let this group of people become part of their needed support system. With vulnerability, Kerry disclosed the illness and shared what immediate support from the group would be helpful. Kerry also identified what else would be helpful in the coming months to stay strong and positive. One of those things was drawing strong boundaries to protect the time needed to attend to their health.

One year after the initial diagnosis, Kerry reported that all things pointed to a full recovery and that the congregation's ministry was feeling stronger because members stepped up in the crisis and were now taking more responsibility for ministry on a daily basis. And probably best of all, Kerry felt stronger and more ready to handle whatever would be thrown at them in the future.

FOR REFLECTION

- To what part of Kerry's story do you relate?
- What life habits have you developed that contribute to your ability to be resilient?

On our path to belonging, we've discussed cognitive strategies, spirituality, the essentials of belonging itself, and wisdom. We'd be remiss if we didn't talk at least briefly about resilience. The truth is that all the practices we've discussed in the path to belonging are about resilience, but we haven't explicitly named them as such and desire to put a finer point on it.

First, what is resilience? Merriam-Webster simply defines resilience as "the ability to become strong, healthy, or successful again after something bad happens."[1] Matt Bloom, the author of *Flourishing in Ministry*, whom we've introduced you to in other parts of the book, defines resilience as "our capacity to adapt, change, and respond to life's challenges and also our capacity to grow, learn, and develop new capabilities and capacities."[2] In this chapter, we offer some additional information about resilience that hasn't already been covered and about how, in our experience, it relates to loneliness.

Why is resilience, the ability to bounce back from adversity, important as we think about loneliness? Resilience, like wisdom, is negatively correlated with loneliness. People with more resilience are less likely to report feelings of loneliness. It turns out that resilience is an important contributor to a good quality of life as we age. A 2017 study on resilience, loneliness, mental health, and the quality of life in old age showed that more resilient older adults have better mental health and less loneliness.[3] So having a healthy level of resilience is good insurance for quality of life as we age. But resilience is also a set of practices or habits we build over time, so we shouldn't wait until we're seventy to try to become more resilient!

RESILIENCE BASICS FOR CLERGY

In 2020, Andrea Sielaff, Kate Davis, and Derek McNeil of the Seattle School of Theology and Psychology completed an extensive literature review of clergy resilience research over the previous twenty-five years.[4] Based on their reading of the studies, they wisely note that clergy resilience involves the interaction of three factors: congregational support, denominational support, and practices by the clergyperson. When these factors come together, a minister's resilience increases dramatically. These authors further emphasize that a clergyperson can do a lot on their own to bolster their resilience—independent of congregational or denominational support—by taking the following four steps:

- Setting intentional boundaries. Resilient clergy know how to set boundaries that allow time for family and friends, which they identify as their two most important sources of social support. From a Bowen family systems perspective, they further recognize the benefit of emotional differentiation, especially during times of congregational conflict.
- Developing self-awareness. Resilient clergy take intentional steps to increase their emotional intelligence, self-compassion, and awareness of God's grace. Several studies mention mentors, counselors, coaches, spiritual directors, and other confidants as being crucial to the development of self-awareness.
- Participating in spiritual practices. Resilient clergy engage in daily spiritual practices, including solitude, prayer, meditation, fasting, and journaling. The form of spiritual practice matters less than the fact that they participate in one. We'll come back to this topic later in this chapter.

- Participating in peer groups. Resilient clergy regularly seek out the support of colleagues. The research across the decades finds that clergy benefit from meeting with peers in a myriad of ways. Specifically, peer groups serve to validate their experiences, normalize their emotions, and provide opportunities for vicarious learning.

Bloom takes a slightly different approach based on his ongoing study of several thousand clergy. He recommends "three small steps" to building resilience, emphasizing a change in these lifestyle habits: daily relaxation, detachment, and adequate sleep.[5] Bloom elaborates that relaxation means practices that will physically relax the body, such as exercise, walking, or simply taking a fifteen-minute rest during the day. With our clients at LeaderWise, we often recommend progressive muscle relaxation, which is the intentional tensing and releasing of different muscle groups in a systematic way. It's best done with a guide, and numerous possibilities are available on Spotify, YouTube, and various meditation sites.

By detachment, Bloom means engaging in something other than ministry for a brief period of time during the day. Ideally, this activity will absorb your attention fully and give you a break. Some possibilities that Bloom offers are Scripture reading, hymn singing, liturgy, and other spiritual practices. At LeaderWise, we also hear about clergy who detach by calling a friend, reading science fiction, immersing themselves in historical fiction, playing fantasy sports, and engaging in any number of other detachment activities. Any activity that will help your mind relax for even a few minutes does the job.

The final recommendation is sleep, and Bloom cites the research literature that generally recommends seven to nine hours of sleep per night for most people. Numerous studies connect inadequate sleep to increased rates of stress and anxiety, and sleep is a natural step to bringing balance back into our lives.

CIGNA LONELINESS STUDIES
AND RESILIENCE PRACTICES

In their national studies on loneliness, Cigna, a managed health care and insurance company, identifies four behaviors to specifically help alleviate loneliness.[6] While their research was not limited to clergy, the recommended practices validate several of the resilience basics for clergy discussed in the previous section. For each of these behaviors, the Cigna researchers observe that spending the right amount of time—or as they phrase it at points, finding "perfect balance"—makes the behaviors effective. It's also important to note that participants self-report whether they have too much, the right balance, or too little of these characteristics in their life. This means their own perception matters as much as anything. There is no "correct number" for time spent in any of these activities—only that you believe you have the right amount. The researchers identify the following characteristics:

- Getting enough sleep. Those who believe they have the right amount of sleep (i.e., not too much or little) are significantly less likely to report that they lack companionship and more likely to say that they have someone to turn to when needed.
- Spending time with family. Those who report that they spend just the right amount of time with family members are significantly more likely to say that they can find companionship when they need it.
- Participating in physical exercise. Those who perceive that they engage in the right amount of physical exercise feel as though they have a group of friends, have a lot in common with others, and can find companionship when they want it.
- Establishing work/life balance. Those who say they have the right balance between work and other activities in their lives are the least likely to be lonely.

Although this is correlational research, which means that we can't definitively conclude that these behaviors result in less loneliness, the size and scope of the Cigna studies suggest that we should pay attention to them. The results further fit with other literature and research on resilience and resonate with our own experience.

LEADERWISE APPROACH

Loneliness and resilience are two topics we encounter a lot in our work with clergy, and they go hand in hand, given the importance of social connection to physical, emotional, and spiritual health. In our own reading of the scientific research, including the work we discussed previously, we've identified these five elements as essential for resilience and well-being (in rank order) for people in general: social support, anti-rumination strategies (such as cognitive behavioral therapy techniques for keeping things in perspective), physical exercise, sleep, and nutrition. Importantly, when reviewing the research for clergy specifically, we would add spiritual practices and put them at the top of the list. Several studies that focus on clergy find that God-efficacy and God-confidence (i.e., feeling grounded in the Divine), as pointed out by Sielaff, Davis, and McNeil, have real effects on resilience among clergy. Regular spiritual practices alone distinguish highly resilient clergy from their less resilient colleagues. In one study, researchers compared highly resilient ministers, as identified by mental health counselors and denominational staff, to ministers in general based on the ways they coped with the demands of ministry. They found that 66 percent of highly resilient ministers spontaneously identified spiritual practices as important for their emotional health versus 33 percent for ministers overall.[7] Other research has likewise highlighted spiritual practices as being essential for resilience among clergy.[8] In contrast to the resilience literature for the general population, self-efficacy, the belief that one can accomplish a specific task or goal, and self-confidence, a general feeling of competence, didn't surface as being predictive of resilience for clergy.

Each of us needs to find what resilience practices work best for us as individuals. While physical exercise may be an effective stress release for many, others may find that rest or sleep is even more important for them. Which practices will be most effective for you really depends on what resilience practices you have already adopted and what might be missing. For instance, when I (Mark) was finishing up my doctorate, my time was limited because I was working full time, writing a dissertation, and attending to the needs of a young family. I made a conscious choice to sacrifice an extra hour of sleep so I would have time for physical exercise. Decades later, I now have time for both—though I would likely choose sleep at this stage in my life! In our resilience workshops, we encourage each minister to find their own nonnegotiables—those three to five practices that can make the most difference for their well-being.

Bloom, in fact, has a simple exercise called "Map Your Day" that can help identify what contributes to well-being for each of us. At the end of each day, draw a face, either smiling or frowning, to identify whether it was a good or bad day. Briefly record key events of the day, both positive and negative, such as social interactions, ministry responsibilities, and personal activities. When a couple of weeks have passed, review your entries, and look for patterns that contribute to both good and bad days. Going forward, work to incorporate more of the life-giving activities into your day-to-day pursuits.[9] These can become your nonnegotiables.

We began part 2 of this book cautioning you against thinking you have to make *all* of the loneliness remedies we suggest part of your daily life while encouraging you to find one or two ideas that feel doable and start them right away. Our hope is that you have had moments in your reading where you have thought, "I can do that!" Those are the behaviors to experiment with right now. As a matter of fact, when we lead workshops on resilience, we end them by asking people, "What one or two practices can you begin right away?" The "right away" part is important. "Right away" means they are easy and doable, and you don't feel like you'll need to climb a mountain to achieve them. Start there, and you'll begin to find your path to belonging. You undoubtedly have your own ideas about what fills you up, or you can try something from the list we've discussed in this chapter:

- spiritual practice
- social support
- antirumination strategies
- physical exercise
- sleep
- nutrition

Regardless, we invite you with the question "What one or two practices can you begin right away?"

FOR REFLECTION AND DISCUSSION

1. What one or two ideas from this chapter on resilience can you start doing right away?
2. What feelings have come up for you as you've read part 2 of this book?
3. What feels particularly hard? What steps can you take to help with that?

PART III

For Congregations, Denominations, and Judicatories

Throughout this book, as we have discussed the epidemic of loneliness and spoken to clergy about what they can do about personal feelings of loneliness, we have emphasized that well-being isn't a solo act. Humans are social creatures meant to live in community and care for one another. Therefore, if you—as leaders, staff, and members of congregations, denominations, and judicatories—want your clergy to be healthier (including less lonely), then you are a part of the solution. We hope these final two chapters in our book will inspire you to be part of the solution. And if you can be part of the solution for your ministers, then perhaps you can also be part of the solution for the epidemic of loneliness in the general population (and even for yourself). After all, what better place for healing than the church, reimagined and reformed anew into a community where people truly love God and neighbor and increased well-being in society is a tangible result?

What Congregations Can Do

Love your neighbor as yourself.

—Matthew 22:39

Dylan was seventeen years old and living on his own. Given a difficult family situation, he couch surfed from house to house, and several families opened their homes to him. One of these families attended a neighborhood church, and they invited him to join them one Sunday. Dylan experienced an immediate welcome. People of all ages spoke to him, introduced him to their community, and sought to make him feel at ease. He became a regular attendee, participated actively in the youth group, volunteered at the local food pantry, and traveled across the country with congregation members to help out on mission trips.

With confirmation Sunday coming, Dylan wanted to participate in the rite. The minister gave him "a crash course" and then discovered, while talking casually with Dylan the morning of the confirmation service, that he had never been baptized. A half hour before the worship service, the minister quietly and quickly gathered the confirmation class and a few parents for an impromptu baptism.

Kindness begets kindness, and grace, love, and hospitality permeated the community. The church became known in the community as the "friendly church," and more and more visitors attended. Dylan graduated from high school two years later, and as he shared his intention to join the Navy, he thanked the congregation publicly for being "my family and giving me a home."

FOR REFLECTION

- To what part of Dylan's story do you relate?
- Think about a time when your congregation reached out to help someone as tangibly as this congregation helped Dylan. What was the impact on the person and even on you and the rest of the congregation?

If God intends us to be creatures in relationship, then the church's vocation must include creating experiences of beloved belonging and community. In chapter 5, we talked about how difficult it is to find true community. But what if the church, in all its expressions, deeply understood God's vision of relationship and community as central to our lives as people and groups of faith? What if the church then focused its mission on building that community—on being a place of true healing and acceptance? That may be a grand dream on our part, and certainly our focus in this book is on the well-being of clergy, not reforming the whole church on earth. This chapter explores how congregations can be part of the path to belonging for clergy and invites congregations to think about contributing to the well-being of our neighbors across society.

Any effort to build true community starts with one-on-one relationships, especially the relationship between each individual and their clergy and the congregation as a whole and their clergy. If you are a member of a congregation and you are reading this book, our hope is that you picked it up because you care about your minister(s) and want to learn how to support them better. We also hope that you've received many helpful ideas.

Here is our invitation to you. Read this book with your church board or personnel committee or another small group. Discuss how you support your ministers now and where you might have fallen short. Share what you learned and what surprised, humbled, and convicted you as you read this book. Brainstorm ways you could increase your support based on what you've already read. Perhaps initiate a conversation with your minister and ask them what they thought of this book, where they've experienced what they've read here, and how the congregation can support them better.

EMOTIONAL CONTAGION

Congregation leaders and members attend to clergy lone-liness not only out of love for this neighbor. A pastor's (or member's) loneliness can affect the entire congregation. As ministers, we've witnessed many times how emotions are contagious. Clergy often describe their congregations as "friendly," "unfriendly," "joyful," "depressed," "supportive," "complaining," or any number of adjectives. It's as if the whole congregation has one persona. Based on psychological research, we have learned that when enough individual mem-bers feel a particular emotion, it may come to characterize the mood of the community.

In fact, researchers have demonstrated that emotions can be passed from one person to the next. Cacioppo, Christakis, and Fowler accessed the data from the Framingham study, a large epidemiological study that has tracked heart disease across multiple generations, to study social connection and the spread of emotions, both positive and negative.[1] Their research finds that loneliness is highly contagious. If you have a friend who is lonely, there is a 52 percent greater chance that you'll become lonely in the next two years. And then it gets interesting. If you have a friend of a friend who is lonely (two degrees of separation), your odds of experiencing loneliness increase 25 percent, even if you've never met the first per-son in the sequence. Likewise, a friend of a friend of a friend (three degrees of separation) who is lonely will increase your risk of becoming lonely by 15 percent. The researchers' results further indicate that friends rather than family members have a much greater impact on our risk for loneliness.

With regard to church, the power of friends' emotions potentially amplifies the mood contagion effect because many church attendees count other church members to be among their friends. If our friends are lonely, we're also more likely to be lonely. This finding likely applies to clergy serving a congregation with lonely people too. Cacioppo, a lead researcher in this study, explains, "When you feel lonely, you have more negative interactions than non-lonely people. If you're in a more negative mood, you're more likely to interact with someone else in a more negative way, and that person is more likely to interact in a negative way."[2] The ripple effect of loneliness spreads throughout the community, potentially including the minister.

The good news is that the contagion effect can apply to positive emotions too. Fowler and Christakis drew upon the same data set to analyze the spread of happiness.[3] Similar to loneliness, their results suggest, the most powerful transmission of happiness occurs among friends rather than family members, and happiness passes through social networks. That is, you have a 15 percent greater chance of happiness over the next two years if a friend is happy, 10 percent for a friend of a friend, and 6 percent for a friend of a friend of a friend. Each additional happy friend in your social network boosts your happiness odds by an additional 9 percent.

BUILDING TRUE COMMUNITY

As introduced in chapter 5, M. Scott Peck says that true communities are characterized by *inclusivity, commitment,* and *consensus.* This is a tall order. Peck says that "groups that exclude others because they are poor or doubters or divorced or sinners or of some different race or nationality are not communities; they are cliques—actually defensive bastions against community."[4] True *inclusivity,* on the other hand, is always seeking to expand. In the case of the church, the purpose of expansion isn't to get more money or to have more people in worship but to love the neighbor, regardless of any return on that investment and regardless of who the neighbor is, for the *expansion* of God's love in the world. Being inclusive isn't something you can fake or trick. And it can be a challenge for congregations that are worried about a decline in the number of people in worship or about keeping the lights and heat on. If you, as a leader or member, truly wish your congregation to expand, it has to be for the sake of true inclusivity.

Commitment is about the desire to stay in relationship, no matter what. When we marry, we verbalize our commitment to the other for better or worse, in sickness and health, until death do us part. What would such a commitment look like in a church? It would mean working together to vulnerably and honestly solve differences, to learn anew daily what it means to love God and our neighbors, and then to stand shoulder to shoulder to do just that, even when it feels hard. At LeaderWise, when we accompany congregations in conflict, sometimes when the process gets hard the system quits. People dig in their heels, leave, or simply refuse to cooperate. But that's not ideally how committed relationships work. In committed relationships, when the going gets tough, we dig in our heels, not in obstinate refusal to participate, but in adamant determination to work out the issues. Just imagine if we could learn how to do this well in our churches, how churches might then be a place where society learns to solve problems well also.

It's difficult to know what to say about the *consensus* Peck has identified. As a nation and a church, we are familiar and comfortable with majority rule decision-making. Groups can learn to make decisions in other ways, however. We know of a church in Minneapolis whose members frequently tell a story that describes a core value of the congregation and their culture. The short version of the story goes like this. Like many old and beautiful churches, it has beloved stained glass windows that were created and installed during the Great Depression. In addition to telling the story of the Gospel, the windows tell a story about a group of people committed to Christ and one another by virtue of the fact that the windows were created during this tumultuous time.

Later, there came a movement to purchase and install a pipe organ. One man was very against the organ, in part because its installation would cover up one of the stained glass windows that meant so much to this congregation. He was outspoken about it and worked hard to use his influence to tamp down the growing desire for the organ. A congregational meeting was called, and he spoke passionately about all the reasons they should not take this step. The congregation voted, and as the tallies revealed that the congregation wanted to proceed with the organ purchase, this man immediately wrote the first and biggest check. This scenario might not, by definition, demonstrate consensus. But if churches can achieve this type of all-for-one behavior, it will have the same effect as consensus.

Dear congregation leaders and members, this is an appeal to you to imagine how you can become places of true community. First, support your clergy in ways you imagine after having read this book. Second, rethink what it means to be a person of faith. In our work with Christian churches in crisis, we have heard time and time again platitudes such as "Christians just don't behave that way" or "We can't argue because Christians don't do that" or "We can't fire that person because that's not Christian." Many places of worship have created a damaging myth—that Christians are 100 percent saint, 0 percent sinner. Perhaps that myth is at work in other faith traditions too. Regardless, it just isn't true. If it were true, we would not feel like these are places where we belong. We wouldn't want to be there because we would know we couldn't measure up to the community's mythical standards. We need faith communities to become places where we can safely, vulnerably express what it means to be human—warts, sins, and all. We also need to understand deeply that clergy are human. They have feelings and needs, and they also make mistakes. Finally, we need to learn how to stay in healthy conflict with one another so we can live in healthy relationship together too. If we can do that, faith communities might again become centers of change for a more positive society.

TEACHING WISDOM

In times past, religious institutions were often the source of education for communities. While churches certainly can't be the providers of all the education one needs to make one's way in life, churches can teach wisdom, and if churches can do that, we might just experience a less lonely society. In his book *Wiser: The Scientific Roots of Wisdom, Compassion, and What Makes Us Good*, American geriatric neuropsychiatrist Dilip Jeste says that, in our quest to make faster progress in technical and scientific industries, our educational systems stopped teaching "fine arts" education in favor of technical, knowledge-based education. This shift has left us with declining wisdom. He says, "We must find ways to infuse the education of our young with lessons that promote the elements of wisdom: compassion and other prosocial behaviors, self-reflection, emotional regulation, openness to divergent perspectives, and ability to make good decisions."[5]

Imagine if our churches infused these wisdom elements in all ministries as part of what it means to love God, love self, and love the neighbor. Imagine if our adult education hours taught about the more nuanced parts of wisdom, such as emotional intelligence, and how to have respectful difficult conversations. With the significant correlation between wisdom and lack of feelings of loneliness, which we explored in chapter 7, not only would we all feel less lonely if churches could teach wisdom, but we would also improve society as a whole.

We, your authors, believe that God isn't done with God's church yet. We also firmly believe that the church of the future is one in which lonely people, among all the people, are fully accepted and loved for who they are. Finally, we believe that those churches that fully and truly live out the command to love their neighbor (inside and outside the walls of the church) will not only survive but also thrive. It is the vocation of each congregation to ask the question "What does this mean *for us?*" and then go about creating the appropriate ministry.

Congregations aren't the only expressions of the church that can help turn the tables on clergy (and societal) loneliness. Denominations and judicatories can also help. And we turn our attention there in the next and final chapter.

FOR REFLECTION AND DISCUSSION

1. As a congregation leader or member, what emotional mood do you think prevails in your congregation? Why do you think that?

2. What letter grades would you give your congregation for inclusivity, commitment, and consensus?

3. What can you, as a congregation leader or member, do to support your ministers more?

10

A Word to Denominations and Judicatories

The isolation clergy feel is real and will not dissipate unless support systems are built into the structure of their denominational hierarchy and polity.

—E. Wayne Hill, Carol Anderson Darling, and Nikki M. Raimondi, "Understanding Boundary-Related Stress in Clergy Families"

I (Mary Kay) was in my early days of ministry. I was having a conversation with a judicatory staff person over coffee early one morning. Prior to entering ministry, I was a leadership coach and consultant and had spent years accompanying and supporting leaders as they tried to direct people and lead change initiatives in their sector of the world. Much of my coaching focused on equipping and building up confidence in

165

the leaders I was accompanying. They needed support from outside the structures of their organizations.

In my conversation with one client, Rita, I asked where clergy are expected to turn when they need support. She shared with me that they are encouraged to reach out to their judicatories for all their needs. I was, to quote Winnie the Pooh, "confuzzled," because I couldn't imagine taking my problems to the staff that held the keys to my next call (as is the case in my denomination).

FOR REFLECTION

- To what part of this story do you relate?
- For judicatory leaders, how can you provide your clergy support without getting into a dual-role bind with them?

When the judicatory leaders and staff hold the key to the clergyperson's current and next call, the dual role of support and oversight complicates the relationship and often creates a barrier between the two. Ministers are hesitant to lay bare to their judicatory all that's happening for them in their work. But clergy can't turn to their congregation or staff for support either, given their need to hold clear boundaries.

That being said, denominational and judicatory leaders and staff can support their clergy and begin to alleviate experiences of isolation and loneliness. In this chapter, we share some of our ideas on this topic with the hope that it invites you to think deeply about these and brainstorm other ways to support your ministers.

OFFER OPPORTUNITIES TO WORSHIP

Leading worship week in and week out does not offer the worship leaders an opportunity to encounter God in the same way that it does for those people sitting in the pews. Ministers are constantly worried about the details, making sure everything is just right so their congregations can encounter our living, loving God. Judicatory leaders can provide worship services for their clergy that are explicitly for the clergy's edification and not included in any other required event. These services would be intended to fill the souls of their ministers and also provide opportunities for clergy to connect personally with colleagues—a double win.

PROMOTE CONTINUING EDUCATION, WELL-BEING WORK, AND SABBATICALS

Clergy, being givers first, don't like to ask for what they need. Therefore, they don't often seek the support they need. Denominations and judicatories can be proactive, as suits their polity. First, encourage or even pressure congregations to provide sufficient continuing education money in their budgets. The money should be available to be used at the pastor's discretion—for leadership development programs, counseling, spiritual direction, coaching, or other support systems and groups. Second, denominations or judicatories should establish a pool of funds that clergy in congregations that truly can't afford to support their ministers in this way can draw on to attend to their own well-being.

Most judicatories require their clergy to take boundary training courses periodically. At LeaderWise, we continually hear stories from our boundary training class participants about how impactful the training was—that taking time to consider their own well-being and ministry was helpful. Normally, judicatories require boundaries training every three to five years. Some of our clients are now requiring the training each year. Regardless of the frequency, we urge judicatories to require periodic boundaries training, make sure it is well designed and guided by skilled leaders, and provide the funds for it so clergy don't have to use their continuing education funds for this important training.

Next, judicatory leaders can also teach congregations what appropriate support of the minister looks like. For example, they can help congregations understand what good clergy boundaries are and why we promote them (see chapter 3). They can have conversations with congregation leaders around their expectations of clergy and guide congregations to reset them when expectations are unrealistic. This kind of education with congregations is ideally done during pastoral transition times but can be done in many ways throughout a minister's tenure.

Sabbaticals can be lifelines for clergy—times of reflection and renewal. We encourage judicatory teams to create sample sabbatical policies and urge congregations to adopt them. Further, judicatories can promote the benefits of sabbaticals as they are in conversation with congregations about other matters, again particularly during pastoral transitions.

A Lutheran synod in the Midwest created a sabbatical team that wrote a sabbatical policy, raised money to support clergy who want to take sabbaticals, visited congregations to talk about the importance of sabbatical, and helped clergy and congregations create sabbatical plans. The team explained that these sabbatical plans weren't just for the clergy. They were also for the congregation; that is, the clergy's time away was also a sabbatical time for the congregation, so wise congregation leaders would create a plan to use that time well.

OFFER CLERGY PEER GROUPS

Social support in the company of people who "get" what we do is so important for clergy (see chapter 6). We know some judicatories that have organized (and supported monetarily) peer groups within the ranks of their ministers and then have gotten out of the way. Each peer group determines what it wants and needs, with no reporting back to the judicatory except to indicate that they are meeting and that the groups are beneficial and to ask for monetary support. Creating a system of peer groups is again a way for judicatories to let their ministers know they care about and support them.

PROVIDE PASTORAL REFLECTIVE SUPERVISION

We introduced you to reflective supervision in chapter 5. The supervision space is a trusted, holy, and confidential place for clergy to explore all they experience in ministry. The Methodist Church in Britain (MCB) found that having clergy in supervision is emotionally rich as well as a benefit to the denomination. Clergy experienced an increased sense of belonging and increased confidence, among other benefits. Supervisees shared that they felt less isolated and less stressed.[1] How might judicatories create programs of reflective supervision for all clergy in their system? To explore this more deeply, we highly recommend reading Jane Leach's book, *A Charge to Keep: Reflective Supervision and the Renewal of Christian Leadership.*

These are just a few ways denominations and judicatories can support their clergy. We are confident that given some time to listen and to brainstorm, leaders and staff can come up with a whole host of additional ways to support clergy.

A final word. We, your authors, feel deep gratitude for all you clergy who are so committed to your vocation and are feeling a deep sense of isolation. We hope that after reading this book, you realize you are not alone and that even that realization can help you feel less isolated. We are grateful for congregations who support their clergy in helpful, boundaried ways so clergy have the support they need to be the best ministers possible. And we are deeply grateful for denominational and judicatory staff who have found innovative ways to support all the ministers in their midst. Our hope, prayer, and belief is that all expressions of the church can be the source and center for healing in society and that you, regardless of your role in the broad expression of church, will begin to ask the question "How can we make a difference here?"

FOR REFLECTION AND DISCUSSION

1. What have you, as a denomination or judicatory leader or staff member, done to help your clergy overcome feelings of loneliness and isolation?
2. What additional support could you offer?

Appendix

LeaderWise Clergy Loneliness Survey

Our survey uses the UCLA Loneliness Scale (Version 3), which is a state-of-the-art research tool to measure loneliness. It is one of the most widely used research loneliness scales in the field. In addition, we created a demographic form focused on the particularities of clergy life that enables us to do group-level statistical analyses based on participants' patterns of responses.

Survey of Church Leaders

1. With which of the following groups do you identify professionally? Select all that apply.
   a. American Baptist Churches USA
   b. Converge
   c. The Episcopal Church
   d. Evangelical Lutheran Church in America

e. Church of the Lutheran Brethren

f. Lutheran Church—Missouri Synod

g. Metropolitan Community Churches

h. The Moravian Church in American

i. Presbyterian Church (USA)

j. The Roman Catholic Church

k. Unitarian Universalist Association

l. United Church of Christ

m. The United Methodist Church

n. Inter/Nondenominational

2. Please describe your gender.

3. Please describe your race/ethnicity.

4. What is your age?

5. Are you currently in a romantic relationship with a partner?

    a. I am *not* currently in a romantic relationship with a partner.

    b. I am married (or in a civil union) and living *with* my partner.

    c. I am married (or in a civil union) and living *apart from* my partner.

    d. I am *not* married (or in a civil union) and living *with* my partner.

    e. I am *not* married (or in a civil union) and living *apart from* my partner.

6. Do you have a long-lasting or chronic condition that substantially limits one or more of your

major life activities (your ability to see, hear, or speak; to learn, remember, or concentrate)?

   a. Yes

   b. No

   c. Prefer to not answer

7. Approximately how long have you been in professional ministry?

8. Which of the following best describes your current professional ministry role? Please select one.

   a. Solo minister

   b. Minister / senior minister / head of staff

   c. Associate minister

   d. Minister of education, music, recreation, evangelism, or outreach

   e. Minister of children, youth, family, or adults

   f. Specialized ministry (e.g., hospital/hospice chaplain, campus minister, community minister, counselor)

   g. Judicatory level (staff or executive)

   h. Other (please specify)

9. Which of the following best describes the locale for the church(es) where you serve?

   a. Large city

   b. Suburb adjacent to a large city

   c. Small city or town

   d. Rural area

   e. Does not apply to my professional role

10–29. The following statements describe how people sometimes feel. Please indicate how often you feel the way described (Never, Rarely, Sometimes, Always).

Authors' note: At this point in our loneliness survey, we included the UCLA Loneliness Scale (Version 3), which consists of twenty items. The instrument is intended for researchers, and for our book, we used it to study the loneliness of clergy in general, not to evaluate individual ministers. Sample items include "How often do you feel alone?" and "How often do you feel that your relationships with others are not meaningful?" For more information, see Daniel W. Russell, "UCLA Loneliness Scale (Version 3): Reliability, Validity, and Factor Structure," *Journal of Personality Assessment* 66, no. 1 (1996): 20–40.

30. What specific recommendations do you have for professional clergy who experience loneliness? What have you found to be helpful?

31. Is there anything else that you would like to add about clergy loneliness?

Notes

INTRODUCTION

1 "The Cultural Significance of the American Front Porch," University of Virginia, February 15, 2021, http://xroads.virginia.edu/~CLASS/ am483_97/projects/cook/cultur.htm.

2 Vivek Murthy, *Together: The Healing Power of Human Connection in a Sometimes Lonely World* (New York: Harper Wave, 2020), xv.

3 Murthy, xix.

4 Murthy, 77.

5 Murthy, 79.

6 Shawn Achor et al., "America's Loneliest Workers according to Research," *Harvard Business Review*, March 19, 2018, https://hbr.org/ 2018/03/americas-loneliest-workers-according-to-research.

7 Brené Brown, *Braving the Wilderness: The Quest for True Belonging and the Courage to Stand Alone* (New York: Random House, 2019), 14.

8 John T. Cacioppo and William Patrick, *Loneliness: Human Nature and the Need for Social Connection* (New York: W. W. Norton, 2008), 250.

CHAPTER 1: WHAT IS LONELINESS?

1 Cacioppo and Patrick, 40.

2 Cacioppo and Patrick, 147–48.

3 Alexis de Tocqueville, *Democracy in America* (New York: G. Dearborn, 1835).

4 Brené Brown, "Shame and Vulnerability," *Work of the People*, video, 11:15, accessed March 2, 2022, https://www.theworkofthepeople .com/shame-and-vulnerability.

5 Daniel Perlman and Letitia Anne Peplau, "Loneliness," in *Encyclopedia of Mental Health*, ed. Howard Friedman (San Diego: Academic Press, 1998), 571–81.

CHAPTER 2: THE IMPACT OF LONELINESS

1 Naomi I. Eisenberger, Matthew D. Lieberman, and Kipling D. Williams, "Does Rejection Hurt? An fMRI Study of Social Exclusion," *Science* 302, no. 5643 (October 2003): 290–92, https://doi.org/10.1126/science.1089134.

2 E. Kross et al., "Social Rejection Shares Somatosensory Representations with Physical Pain," *Proceedings of the National Academy of Sciences* 108, no. 15 (2011): 6270–75, https://doi.org/10.1073/pnas.1102693108.

3 C. Nathan DeWall et al., "Acetaminophen Reduces Social Pain," *Psychological Science* 21, no. 7 (2010): 931–37, https://doi.org/10.1177/0956797610374741.

4 Stephanie Cacioppo et al., "A Quantitative Meta-analysis of Functional Imaging Studies of Social Rejection," *Scientific Reports* 3, no. 1 (2013): 1–3, https://doi.org/10.1038/srep02027.

5 Julianne Holt-Lunstad et al., "Loneliness and Social Isolation as Risk Factors for Mortality," *Perspectives on Psychological Science* 10, no. 2 (2015): 227–37, https://doi.org/10.1177/1745691614568352.

6 Holt-Lunstad et al., 234.

7 Julianne Holt-Lunstad, Timothy B. Smith, and J. Bradley Layton, "Social Relationships and Mortality Risk: A Meta-analytic Review," *PLoS Medicine* 7, no. 7 (2010), https://doi.org/10.1371/journal.pmed.1000316.

8 Holt-Lunstad et al., "Loneliness and Social Isolation," 227.

9 Dan Nelson, *LeaderWise Loneliness Survey Results* (n.p.: LeaderWise, 2019).

10 "Loneliness Is at Epidemic Levels in America," Cigna Newsroom, accessed December 6, 2021, https://newsroom.cigna.com/loneliness-in-america.

11 Nelson, *Loneliness Survey*.

12 Louise C. Hawkley, Michael W. Browne, and John T. Cacioppo, "How Can I Connect with Thee? Let Me Count the Ways," *Psychological Science* 16, no. 10 (January 2005): 798–804, https://doi.org/10.1111/j.1467-9280.2005.01617.x; Louise C. Hawkley et al., "The Mental Representation of Social Connections: Generalizability Extended to Beijing Adults," *PLoS One* 7, no. 9 (November 2012), https://doi.org/10.1371/journal.pone.0044065; Mark Shevlin, Siobhan Murphy, and Jamie Murphy, "The Latent Structure of Loneliness,"

Assessment 22, no. 2 (2014): 208–15, https://doi.org/10.1177/1073191114542596.

13 Nelson, *Loneliness Survey.*

14 Julianne Holt-Lunstad, "The Double Pandemic of Social Isolation and Covid-19: Cross-Sector Policy Must Address Both: Health Affairs Blog," Health Affairs, June 22, 2020, https://www.healthaffairs.org/do/10.1377/hblog20200609.53823/full/.

15 Holt-Lunstad, Smith, and Layton, "Social Relationships."

16 Holt-Lunstad et al., "Loneliness and Social Isolation," 227–37.

CHAPTER 3: THE CLERGY LIFE

1 Jerrold S. Greenberg, *Comprehensive Stress Management* (Dubuque, IA: William C. Brown, 1990), 295.

2 CBC/Radio Canada, "Study Proves Beatles Right: All You Need Is Love," CBC News, August 4, 2009, https://www.cbc.ca/news/science/study-proves-beatles-right-all-you-need-is-love-1.813624.

3 E. Wayne Hill, Carol Anderson Darling, and Nikki M. Raimondi, "Understanding Boundary-Related Stress in Clergy Families," *Marriage & Family Review* 35, nos. 1–2 (2003): 147–66.

4 Hill, Darling, and Raimondi, 155.

5 Hill, Darling, and Raimondi, 156.

6 Hill, Darling, and Raimondi, 156.

7 Matt Bloom, *Flourishing in Ministry: How to Cultivate Clergy Wellbeing* (Lanham, MD: Rowman & Littlefield, 2019), 91–100.

8 Bloom, 95–96.

9 Chris Adams, "Flourishing in Ministry" (presentation, Ministry Development Council Annual Meeting, New Orleans, LA, January 15, 2020).

PART 2: PATHS TO BELONGING

1 Martin E. Seligman and Mihaly Csikszentmihalyi, "Positive Psychology: An Introduction," *American Psychologist* 55, no. 1 (2000): 5–6, https://doi.org/10.1037/0003-066x.55.1.5, 5–6.

2 Barbara L. Fredrickson, "The Broaden-and-Build Theory of Positive Emotions," *Philosophical Transactions of the Royal Society of London. Series B: Biological Sciences* 359, no. 1449 (2004): 1375, https://doi.org/10.1098/rstb.2004.1512.

3 Fredrickson, 1375.

CHAPTER 4: LEARNING TO THINK DIFFERENTLY

1 "Loneliness Is at Epidemic Levels."
2 Philip Hyland et al., "Can the REBT Theory Explain Loneliness? Theoretical and Clinical Applications," *Cognitive Behaviour Therapy* 48, no. 1 (May 2018): 39–51, https://doi.org/10.1080/16506073.2018.1475505.
3 Christopher M. Masi et al., "A Meta-analysis of Interventions to Reduce Loneliness," *Personality and Social Psychology Review* 15, no. 3 (2010): 219–66, https://doi.org/10.1177/1088868310377394.
4 Paul Ekman and Richard J. Davidson, *The Nature of Emotion: Fundamental Questions* (Cambridge: Oxford University Press, 1994), 56.
5 Tara Brach, "Download Rain: A Practice of Radical Compassion," Tara Brach, September 9, 2020, https://www.tarabrach.com/download-rain-a-practice-of-radical-compassion/.
6 Martin Seligman, *Learned Optimism* (London: Nicholas Brealey, 2018), 220–23.
7 Thich Nhat Hanh, "Who Am I?," Thich Nhat Hanh Dharma Talks, August 13, 2014, https://tnhaudio.org/2014/08/13/who-am-i/.
8 "How Much DNA Do Humans Share with Other Animals?," DNA Tests, accessed December 14, 2021, https://thednatests.com/how-much-dna-do-humans-share-with-other-animals/.

CHAPTER 5: THE ESSENTIALS OF BELONGING

1 Roy F. Baumeister and Mark R. Leary, "The Need to Belong: Desire for Interpersonal Attachments as a Fundamental Human Motivation," *Psychological Bulletin* 117, no. 3 (1995): 497–529.
2 Michelle H. Lim et al., "Introducing a Dual Continuum Model of Belonging and Loneliness," *Australian Journal of Psychology* 73, no. 1 (2021): 81.
3 Lim et al., 84.
4 Brown, *Braving the Wilderness*, 40.
5 Brown, 36.
6 Kristin Neff, Self-Compassion, https://self-compassion.org.
7 Brown, *Braving the Wilderness*, 59.
8 Brown, 64.
9 Brown, 89. While the BS word might sound crass to you, Brown makes a distinction between a lie and BS. A person who lies actually does pay attention to the truth, but a bullshitter ignores truth altogether.
10 "Strong back, soft front" comes out of the Buddhist tradition.

11 M. Scott Peck, *The Different Drum: Community Making and Peace* (New York: Touchstone, 1998), 59.
12 Peck, 61–64.
13 Peck, 60–61.
14 Peck, 62.
15 Julene K. Johnson et al., "Community Choir Intervention to Promote Well-Being among Diverse Older Adults: Results from the Community of Voices Trial," *Journals of Gerontology: Series B* 75, no. 3 (March 2020): 549–59, https://doi.org/10.1093/geronb/gby132.
16 Niklas K. Steffens et al., "Social Group Memberships in Retirement Are Associated with Reduced Risk of Premature Death: Evidence from a Longitudinal Cohort Study," *BMJ Open* 6, no. 2 (2016): e010164, https://doi.org/10.1136/bmjopen-2015-010164.
17 Bloom, *Flourishing in Ministry*, 82.
18 Bloom, 83–84.
19 Bloom, 89.
20 Jane Leach, *A Charge to Keep: Reflective Supervision and the Renewal of Christian Leadership* (Nashville: General Board of Higher Education and Ministry, 2020), 2.
21 Leach, 12.
22 Leach, 52–53.
23 Leach, 53.

CHAPTER 6: THE SPIRITUALITY CONNECTION

1 Michelle Brubaker, "Is Spirituality a Component of Wisdom?," UC San Diego News Center, October 22, 2020, https://ucsdnews.ucsd.edu/pressrelease/is-spirituality-a-component-of-wisdom.
2 Henri J. M. Nouwen, *Reaching Out: The Three Movements of the Spiritual Life* (New York: Image, 1975), 34.
3 Murthy, *Together*, 9.
4 Henri J. M. Nouwen, *The Lonely Search for God*, read by the author (Bethesda, MD: Now You Know Media, 2016), audiobook, 2:28.
5 Henri J. M. Nouwen, *Out of Solitude: Three Meditations on the Christian Life* (Notre Dame, IN: Ave Maria, 2004), 18.
6 Nouwen, 11.
7 Christopher R. Long and James R. Averill, "Solitude: An Exploration of Benefits of Being Alone," *Journal for the Theory of Social Behavior* 33, no. 1 (2003): 21–44.
8 John O'Donohue, *To Bless the Space between Us: A Book of Blessings* (New York: Doubleday, 2008), 112.
9 Robert A. Emmons, Michael E. McCullough, and Philip C. Watkins, "Gratitude and Subjective Well-Being," in *The*

Psychology of Gratitude, ed. Robert A. Emmons and Michael E. McCullough (New York: Oxford University Press, 2004), 167–92. Although early research was promising, recent meta-analyses, which combine the results of several studies, indicate only a small to moderate impact of gratitude practices on well-being and loneliness. Authors cite small sample sizes and the difficulty in measuring gratitude as limitations. At the same time, these researchers do not dismiss gratitude as an intervention and recommend ongoing research. In our work with clergy, we have witnessed the power of gratitude as a helpful intervention for many people (including ourselves), and it resonates deeply with clergy and their spiritual traditions. For this reason, we recommend that our readers give the practice of gratitude a try.

10   Kelly Yu-Hsin Liao and Chih-Yuan Weng, "Gratefulness and Subjective Well-Being: Social Connectedness and Presence of Meaning as Mediators," *Journal of Counseling Psychology* 65, no. 3 (April 2018): 390.

11   Robert A. Emmons, Michael E. McCullough, and Barbara Fredrickson, "Gratitude, like Other Positive Emotions, Broadens and Builds," in Emmons and McCullough, *Psychology of Gratitude*, 145–66.

12   Andrea Caputo, "The Relationship between Gratitude and Loneliness: The Potential Benefits of Gratitude for Promoting Social Bonds," *Europe's Journal of Psychology* 11, no. 2 (2015): 323–34, https://doi.org/10.5964/ejop.v11i2.826; Esther Frinking et al., "Gratitude and Loneliness in Adults over 40 Years: Examining the Role of Psychological Flexibility and Engaged Living," *Aging & Mental Health* 24, no. 12 (August 2019): 2117–24, https://doi.org/10.1080/13607863.2019.1673309.

13   David Steindl-Rast, *Gratefulness, the Heart of Prayer: An Approach to Life in Fullness* (Mahwah, NJ: Paulist, 1984), 204.

14   Glenn Berkenkamp, "Treat Yourself to a Gratitude Walk," Gratefulness.org, October 19, 2020, https://gratefulness.org/resource/treat-yourself-to-an-immune-boosting-mood-elevating-gratitude-walk/.

15   Eric Jaffe, "The Psychological Study of Smiling," Association for Psychological Science, February 11, 2011, https://www.psychologicalscience.org/observer/the-psychological-study-of-smiling.

16   Pema Chödrön, "Six Kinds of Loneliness," *Lion's Roar Blog*, July 30, 2020, accessed August 10, 2020, http://www.lionsroar.com/six-kinds-of-loneliness.

17   Chödrön.

18   Chödrön.

19 Cendri A. Hutcherson, Emma Seppala, and James Gross, "Loving-Kindness Meditation Increases Social Connectedness," *Emotion* 8, no. 5 (2008): 720–24.

20 Jack Kornfield, "Meditation on Lovingkindness," Jack Kornfield, October 21, 2019, https://jackkornfield.com/meditation-on-lovingkindness/.

CHAPTER 7: BEING WISE ABOUT LONELINESS

1 Igor Grossmann and Anna Dorfman, "Wise Reasoning in an Uncertain World," in *Applying Wisdom to Contemporary World Problems*, ed. Robert J. Sternberg, Howard C. Nusbaum, and Judith Glück (Cham, Switzerland: Palgrave Macmillan, 2019), 54.

2 Dilip V. Jeste and Scott LaFee, *Wiser: The Scientific Roots of Wisdom, Compassion, and What Makes Us Good* (Boulder, CO: Sounds True, 2020), 12–15. At LeaderWise, we talk about emotional intelligence as the foundation of many things, including resilience and wisdom. This list of wisdom components includes core components of emotional intelligence (empathy, emotional regulation, and self-reflection, for starters).

3 F. Diane Barth, "To Fight Loneliness, Research Says to Turn to Wisdom," *Psychology Today*, February 24, 2021, https://www.psychologytoday.com/us/blog/the-couch/202102/fight-loneliness-research-says-turn-wisdom.

4 Center for Healthy Aging, "Jeste-Thomas Wisdom Index," UC San Diego Health Sciences, October 12, 2021, https://medschool.ucsd.edu/research/aging/research/Pages/SD-WISE.aspx.

5 Judith Glück, "The Development of Wisdom during Adulthood," in *The Cambridge Handbook of Wisdom*, ed. Robert J. Sternberg and Judith Glück (Cambridge: Cambridge University Press, 2019), 323–45.

6 Robert J. Sternberg, "Why Smart People Can Be So Foolish," *European Psychologist* 9, no. 3 (2004): 145–50, https://doi.org/10.1027/1016-9040.9.3.145.

7 Grossmann and Dorfman, "Wise Reasoning," 71–103.

8 Igor Grossmann, Franki Y. H. Kung, and Henri C. Santos, "Wisdom as State versus Trait," in Sternberg and Glück, *Cambridge Handbook of Wisdom*, 249–72.

9 Hannes Zacher and Ute Kunzmann, "Wisdom in the Workplace," in Sternberg, Nusbaum, and Glück, *Applying Wisdom*, 255–92.

CHAPTER 8: RESILIENCE MATTERS

1 *Merriam-Webster Dictionary*, s.v. "resilience," accessed November 1, 2021, https://www.merriam-webster.com/dictionary/resilience.

2 Bloom, *Flourishing in Ministry*, 2.

3   Eva Gerino et al., "Loneliness, Resilience, Mental Health, and Quality of Life in Old Age: A Structural Equation Model," *Frontiers in Psychology* 8 (2017): 1–12, https://doi.org/10.3389/fpsyg.2017.02003.

4   Andrea M. Sielaff, Kate Rae Davis, and J. Derek McNeil, "Literature Review of Clergy Resilience and Recommendations for Future Research," *Journal of Psychology and Theology* 49, no. 4 (2020): 308–23, https://doi.org/10.1177/0091647120968136.

5   Bloom, *Flourishing in Ministry*, 106.

6   "Loneliness Is at Epidemic Levels."

7   Katheryn Rhoads Meek et al., "Maintaining Personal Resiliency: Lessons Learned from Evangelical Protestant Clergy," *Journal of Psychology and Theology* 31, no. 4 (2003): 339–47, https://doi.org/10.1177/009164710303100404.

8   Janice Bell Meisenhelder and Emily N. Chandler, "Frequency of Prayer and Functional Health in Presbyterian Pastors," *Journal for the Scientific Study of Religion* 40, no. 2 (2001): 323–30, https://doi.org/10.1111/0021-8294.00059; Mark R. McMinn et al., "Care for Pastors: Learning from Clergy and Their Spouses," *Pastoral Psychology* 53, no. 6 (2005): 563–81, https://doi.org/10.1007/s11089-005-4821-y.

9   Bloom, *Flourishing in Ministry*, 104.

CHAPTER 9: WHAT CONGREGATIONS CAN DO

1   John T. Cacioppo, James H. Fowler, and Nicholas A. Christakis, "Alone in the Crowd: The Structure and Spread of Loneliness in a Large Social Network," *Journal of Personality and Social Psychology* 97, no. 6 (2009): 977–91, https://doi.org/10.1037/a0016076.

2   John Cacioppo, "Loneliness Is Contagious," interview by Sharon Jayson, *Miami Times*, December 9, 2009, 15, https://www.proquest.com/newspapers/loneliness-is-contagious/docview/363233869/se-2?accountid=351.

3   James H. Fowler and Nicholas A. Christakis, "Dynamic Spread of Happiness in a Large Social Network: Longitudinal Analysis over 20 Years in the Framingham Heart Study," *British Medical Journal* 337, no. a2338 (2008): 1–9.

4   Peck, *Different Drum*, 61.

5   Jeste with LaFee, *Wiser*, 279.

CHAPTER 10: A WORD TO DENOMINATIONS AND JUDICATORIES

1   Leach, *Charge to Keep*, 12.

Recommended Resources

Bloom, Matthew C. *Flourishing in Ministry: How to Cultivate Clergy Wellbeing*. Lanham, MD: Rowman & Littlefield, 2019.

    Matt Bloom and colleagues, researchers at Notre Dame, have examined clergy resilience for several years. Their ongoing study consists of thousands of Protestant ministers. This highly readable book offers insights based on the empirical findings of their study about potential pitfalls for maintaining resilience and recommendations to improve it. We regularly recommend this book to clergy who are interested in establishing resilience practices and increasing their well-being.

Burns, David D. *Feeling Good: The New Mood Therapy*. New York: Quill, 2000.

    This is a go-to cognitive-behavioral self-help book. When a cognitive-behavioral approach is called for with any number of issues—including loneliness, depression, or anxiety—we'll often recommend this book as an easy-to-read introduction. We've had numerous clients describe its approach as transformational for their thinking, moods, and overall well-being. It can be read while working with a therapist or as a stand-alone resource.

Jeste, Dilip, and Scott LaFee. *Wiser: The Scientific Roots of Wisdom, Compassion, and What Makes Us Good.* Boulder, CO: Sounds True, 2020.

Wisdom has long been ethereal and somewhat hard to define. Historically viewed as a philosophical and religious construct, today it can be studied at the biological level, thanks to advancements in neuroscience and neurobiology. Jeste and LaFee teach us about the biology of wisdom and assure us that we can grow wiser by intentionally practicing the behaviors of wisdom.

"MBSR 8-Week Online Live." UMass Memorial Health. https://www.ummhealth.org/umass-memorial-medical-center/services-treatments/center-for-mindfulness/mindfulness-programs/mbsr-8-week-online-live. Accessed December 30, 2021.

Mindfulness-based stress reduction (MBSR) is the gold standard for how to learn and develop a practice of mindfulness. It is an eight-week program that includes a two-and-a-half-hour weekly class and a day of mindfulness toward the end of the course. In this group experience, you'll be introduced to mindfulness through meditation, body scans, yoga, and more. While we would encourage you to take an in-person class if possible, and numerous clinics and individual practitioners offer them, the internet has opened up the possibility of an online experience when that's not an option. The original MBSR program was developed by Jon Kabat-Zinn at UMass, and there is now an online version, the one we recommend here.

Mueller, Wayne. *Sabbath: Finding Rest, Renewal, and Delight in Our Busy Lives*. New York: Bantam, 2000.

I have written in the margin on one of the first pages of this book, "Wisdom requires rest." The ideal of Sabbath is a radical one in this day and age. There are so many benefits—increasing wisdom, reducing loneliness, and feeling more deeply connected to the Divine. In this book, Mueller implores us to seek Sabbath and make it part of the rhythm of our lives. The book offers numerous reflections, followed by exercises to experiment with along the way. Perhaps by inviting this book to accompany you, you will become not only wiser but also less lonely.

Murthy, Vivek. *Together: The Healing Power of Human Connection in a Sometimes Lonely World*. New York: Harper Wave, 2020.

Murthy, in his first tenure as surgeon general, toured the country and discovered how lonely we are in the United States. This very readable and accessible book offers his findings, some history about loneliness, and his suggested ways to overcome the epidemic of loneliness in which we find ourselves.

Neff, Kristin. Self-Compassion. http://self-compassion.org. Accessed December 30, 2021.

This website is the online home of Dr. Kristin Neff, a psychologist who studies self-compassion. The website offers educational resources, inspiration, practices, and more to help you on your journey toward self-compassion.

Putnam, Robert D. *Bowling Alone: The Collapse and Revival of American Community*. Revised and updated ed. New York: Simon & Schuster, 2020.

In astonishing detail, Robert Putnam notes how American society has become fractured and disjointed. People don't meet for social gatherings—for example, join bowling leagues—as much as they used to. The book was first published in 2000, so Putnam's assertion that cable television has led to a lot of the social isolation we are experiencing seems quaint now, but the general thesis of the book rings true today: technology can drive people apart.

Radtke, Kristen. *Seek You: A Journey through American Loneliness*. New York: Pantheon, 2021.

This engaging book is a graphic memoir of one person's journey through loneliness from childhood to adulthood. Using graphic art and words, it interweaves personal experience, cultural influences, and up-to-date research findings of loneliness. While you'll want to read through the entire book, it can also be placed in a waiting room, in a church library or lounge, or on a coffee table in your office. It's a creative and accessible book that someone can just pick up and page through—and it will likely resonate with their experience.

Sanvello. https://www.sanvello.com/. Accessed December 30, 2021.

This website connects to an app on your smartphone, and you can download the app today! If you're interested in a cognitive-behavioral approach to managing difficult emotions—and you're comfortable with technology—this app might be for you. It's highly interactive and provides an array of cognitive-behavioral techniques at your fingertips, including mindfulness, gratitude, and cognitive reframing practices. Another advantage is that it's available twenty-four hours a day, whenever you might benefit from engaging in one of these techniques.

Sood, Amit. *The Mayo Clinic Guide to Stress-Free Living*. Boston: Da Capo Lifelong Books, 2013.

Author Amit Sood is a medical doctor specializing in stress and resilience at the Mayo Clinic in Rochester, MN. In the book, he explores the brain's contribution to stress in our lives. He says that the brain has a default mode of mind wandering and a focused mode of undistracted presence. In today's world, we spend most of our time in the default mode. This highly readable book explores his stress-free living program, which draws from the fields of neuroscience, spirituality, and psychology, among others. The program helps you train your attention and refine your interpretations, with the goal of finding peace, joy, altruism, and resilience.

Standish, Graham. "Congregation for Clergy Worship." Samaritan Counseling-Guidance-Consulting. November 7, 2021. YouTube video, 21:21. https://www.youtube.com/watch?v=7CjILBF3lUc.

Graham Standish is a PCUSA pastor and author of many books for church leaders. He provides weekly opportunities for worship on YouTube.

Steindl-Rast, David. "Welcome to Gratefulness.org: Bringing Gratitude to Life." Gratefulness.org, https://gratefulness.org/. Accessed December 20, 2021.

This website is the online home of David Steindl-Rast, a Benedictine monastic who has devoted much of his life's work to helping others find psychological and spiritual well-being through the practice of gratitude. It includes numerous resources to develop a regular gratitude practice.

University of Chicago Center for Practical Wisdom. https://wisdomcenter.uchicago.edu/. Accessed December 30, 2021.

The Center for Practical Wisdom offers an easily navigable website describing the most current research on wisdom models, theories, and applications. For people just starting to explore the psychology of wisdom, including its applications to leadership, it also provides videos, suggested readings, and other resources. To begin, you might want to browse its "News" section, which is written for a general audience.

Waldinger, Robert. "What Makes a Good Life: Lessons from the Longest Study on Happiness." November 2015. TEDx-BeaconStreet video, 12:37. https://www.ted.com/talks/robert _waldinger_what_makes_a_good_life_lessons_from_the _longest_study_on_happiness.

In this TED Talk, Robert Waldinger, the director of a multidecade longitudinal study at Harvard University, shares the study's major findings and the three major predictors of happiness—all of which relate to our social connectedness. He speaks with warmth and compassion about the importance of relationships in our lives.